Vermeer's
Love Letters

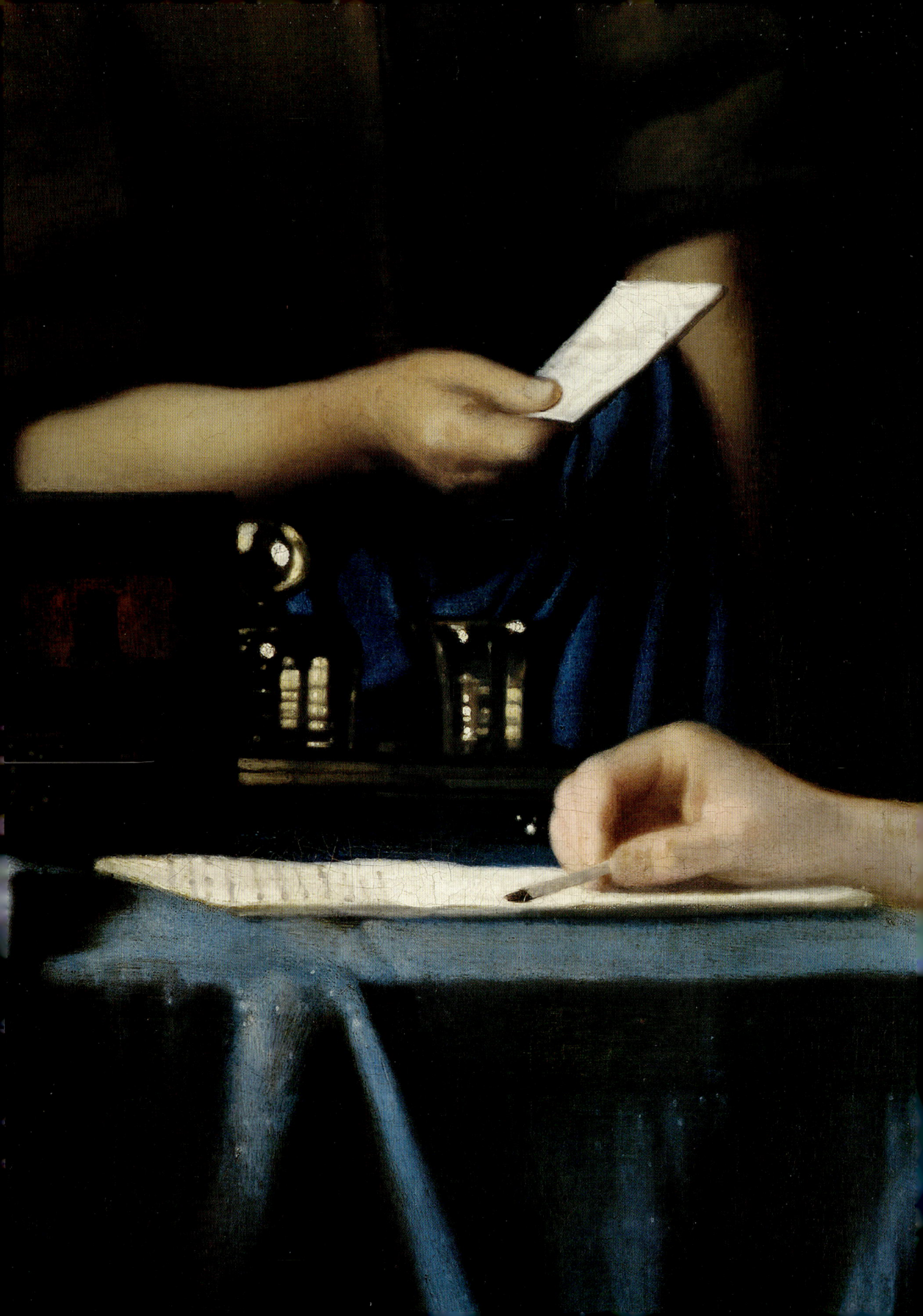

Vermeer's
Love Letters

ROBERT FUCCI

RIZZOLI ELECTA *in association with* THE FRICK COLLECTION

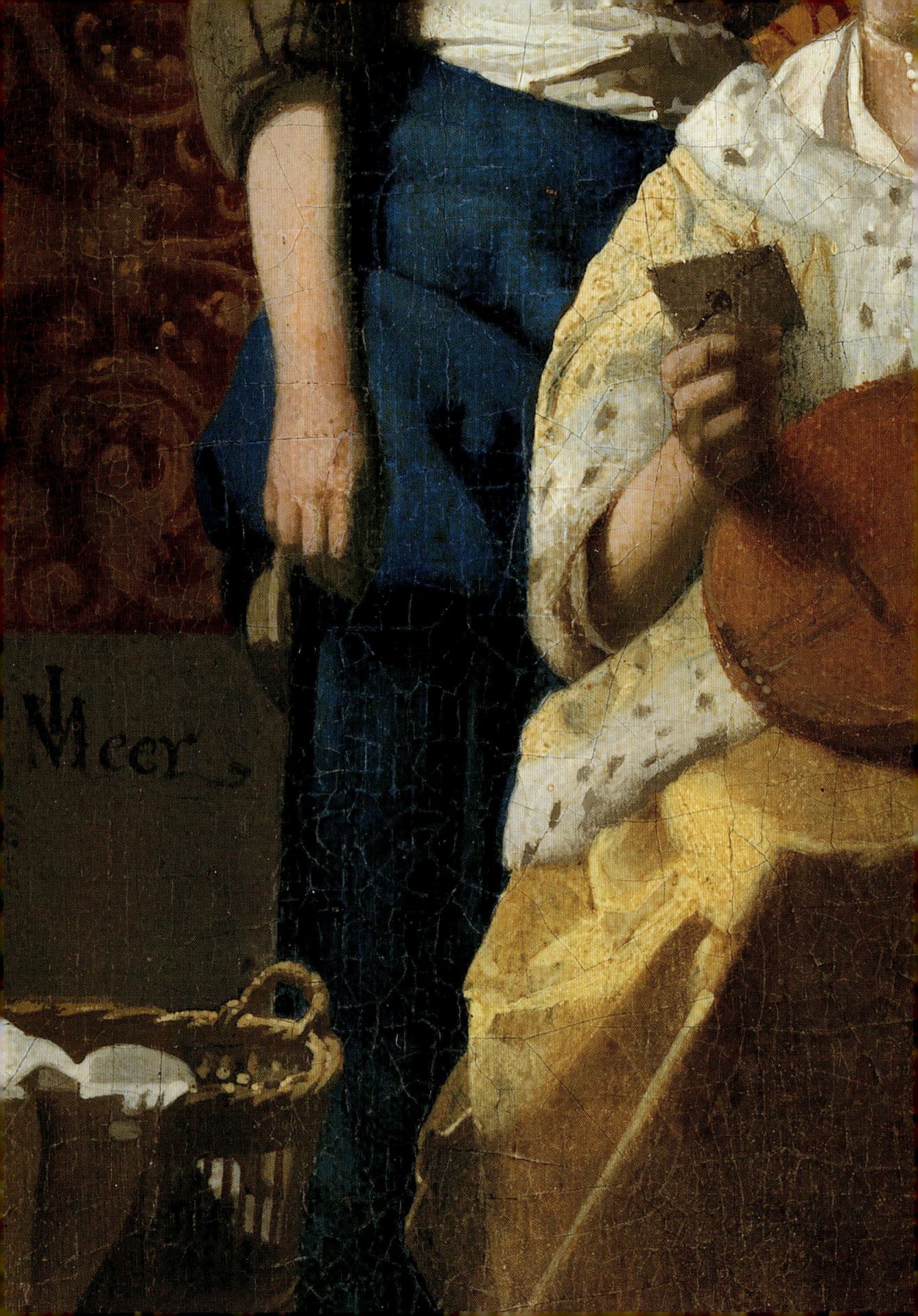

CONTENTS

Director's Foreword

8

Acknowledgments

9

INTRODUCTION

10

CHAPTER 1: *Letters*

14

CHAPTER 2: *Maids*

32

CHAPTER 3: *Modern Love*

50

CHAPTER 4: *Discretion*

66

CATALOGUE

Mistress and Maid

The Love Letter

Woman Writing a Letter with Her Maid

80

Bibliography

102

Index

108

Image Credits

111

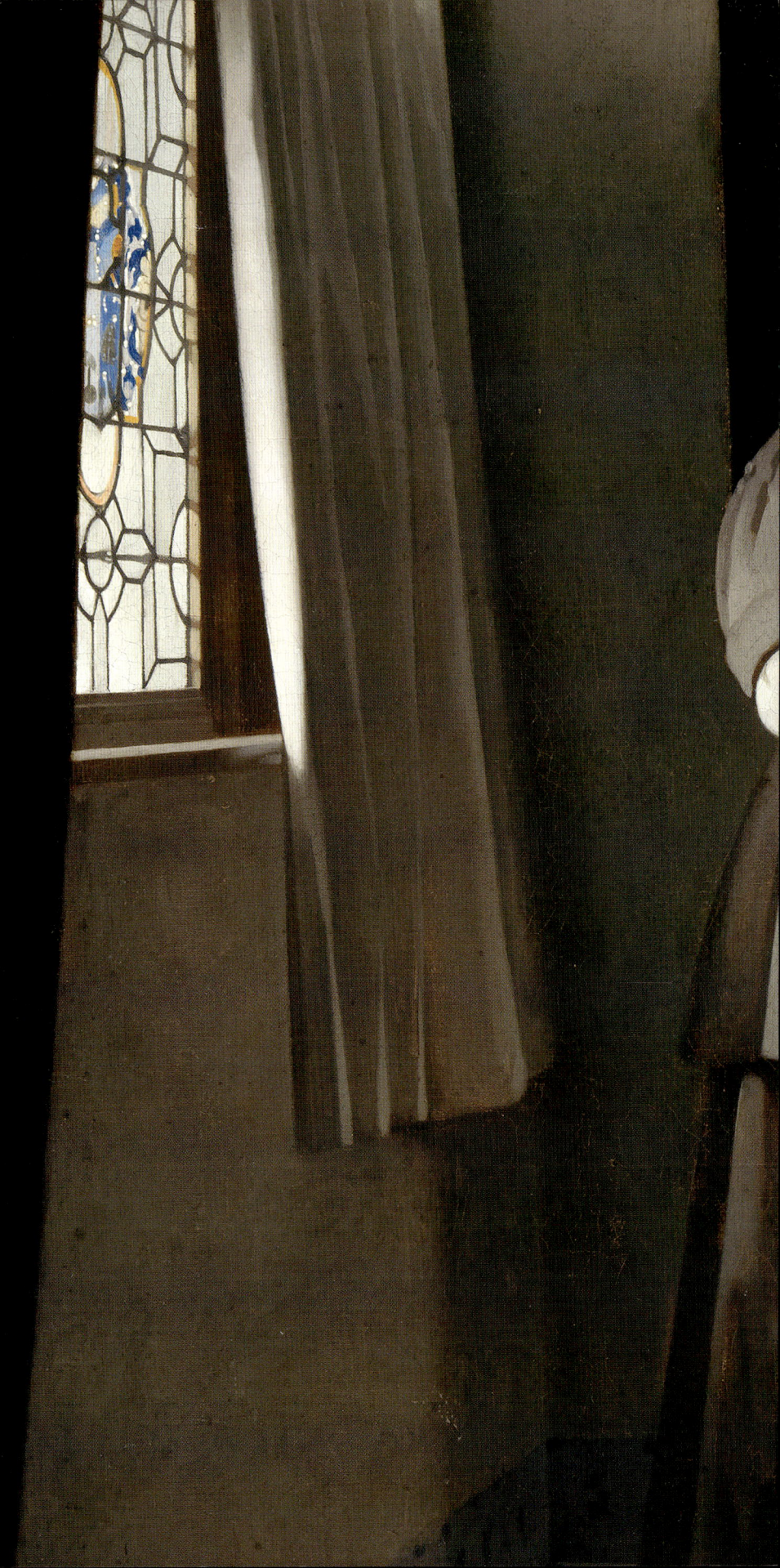

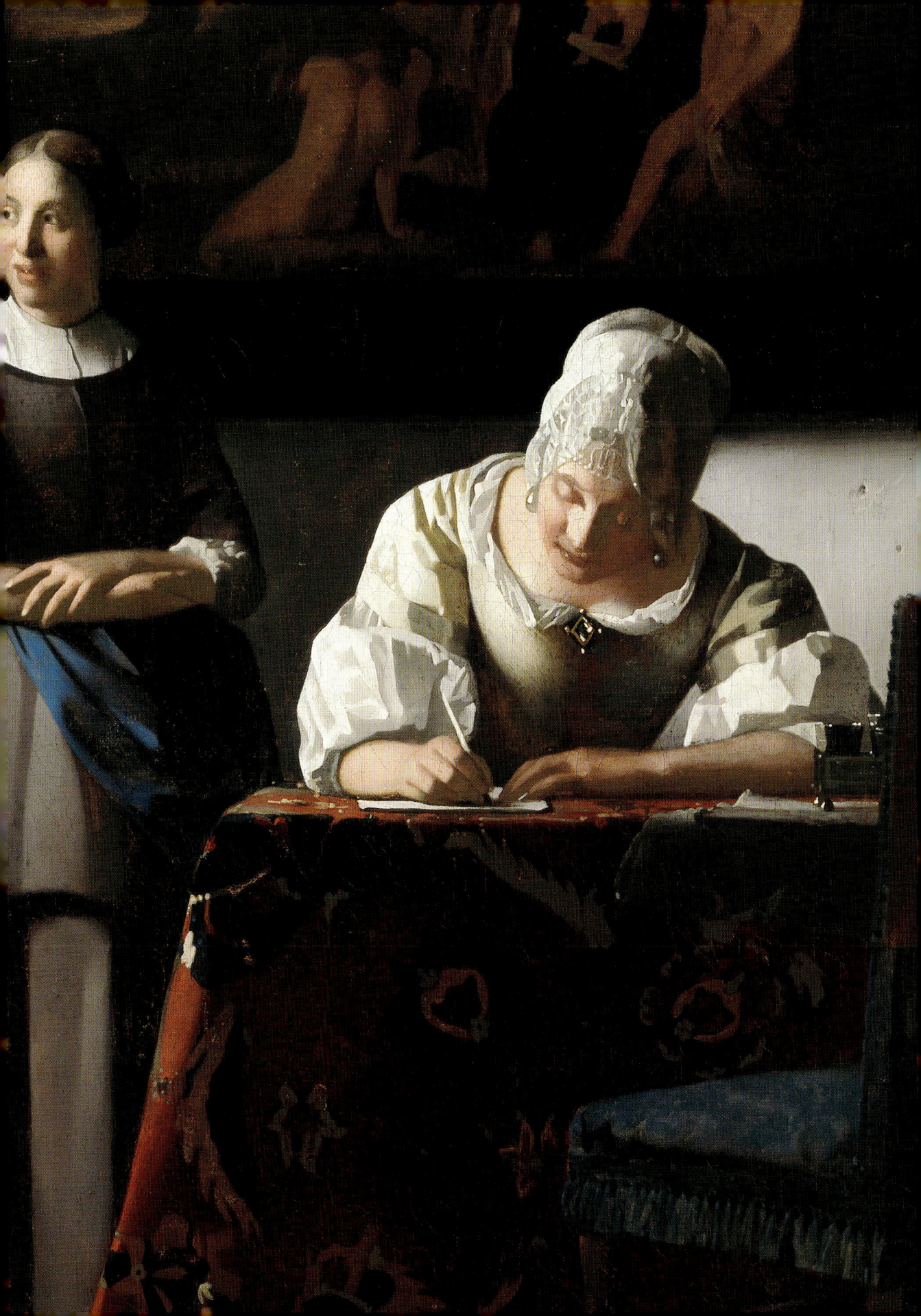

DIRECTOR'S FOREWORD

THIS IS THE FIRST EXHIBITION to be held in The Frick Collection's new Ronald S. Lauder Exhibition Galleries following the museum's reopening after its comprehensive renovation. Having recently taken up the position as director of the Frick, I am particularly pleased to add a few words to the catalogue of this exhibition. *Vermeer's Love Letters* takes its cue from our own *Mistress and Maid* of 1666–67 by the famous Dutch artist and unites it, exceptionally, with two further master-pieces that focus on the alluring motif of writing and receiving letters. The quiet and intimate exchanges between the characters in the paintings still intrigue us today as they touch on questions of communication, personal relationships, secrecy, and emotional connection. In his essay, Robert Fucci, a specialist in seventeenth-century Dutch and Flemish art, brings a fresh perspective to Vermeer's work and these themes. We thank Rob for both his text and his work on the exhibition.

We want to acknowledge the generosity of Ronald S. Lauder, for whom the newly built gallery spaces are named, as well as the Jasmine Charity Trust, whose funding, in memory of Regina Jaglom Wachter, made possible this publication and the exhibition it accompanies. For his essential role in securing this exceptional support, and for so much more, all due credit and heartfelt thanks go to my esteemed predecessor, Ian Wardropper.

We are deeply grateful to the lenders to the exhibition for these exceptional loans. They would not have been possible without the generous support of our colleagues Taco Dibbits, Director, and Pieter Roelofs, Curator, at the Rijksmuseum, and Director Caroline Campbell at the National Gallery of Ireland. At the Frick, thanks go to Xavier F. Salomon, Deputy Director and Peter Jay Sharp Chief Curator; Aimee Ng, John Updike Curator; and the Board of Trustees. We are very grateful to Editor in Chief Michaelyn Mitchell, who managed the production of the catalogue and, with Assistant Editor Gemma McElroy, expertly edited the texts. Others to whom we extend our thanks include Tia Chapman, Joseph Coscia Jr., Allison Galea, Lisa Goble, Joseph Godla, Caitlin Henningsen, Patrick King, George Koelle, Alexis Light, Sara Muskulus, Christopher Roberson, Heidi Rosenau, April Kim Tonin, and Sean Troxell, along with the entire staff of the museum, all of whom contributed in one way or another to the realization of this project. We are also indebted to exhibition designer Patrick Herron, lighting designer Anita Jorgensen, Senior Editor Philip Reeser at Rizzoli, and Sarah Gifford, for her design of this book.

This is the first exhibition in New York City since 2001 of works by one of the most famous artists in the world, Johannes Vermeer, and it seems fitting that this is the inaugural exhibition of the Frick's new Ronald S. Lauder Exhibition Galleries. We hope to bring exhibitions to these spaces that are equally exciting and inspiring for our audiences for years to come.

AXEL RÜGER
Anna-Maria and Stephen Kellen Director
The Frick Collection

ACKNOWLEDGMENTS

I AM DEEPLY GRATEFUL for the vision and efforts of Xavier F. Salomon, Deputy Director and Peter Jay Sharp Chief Curator, who initiated this project. Xavier has been generous and thoughtful throughout the process of shepherding this publication and the exhibition it accompanies. Among the excellent team at The Frick Collection, my thanks also go to Aimee Ng, John Updike Curator, for her help along the way and to Michaelyn Mitchell, Editor in Chief, for her outstanding editorial eye and for seeing this project through.

Essential help and feedback during various phases have also come from Aneta Georgievska-Shine, Lizzie Marx, Pieter Roelofs, Peter Sutton, Gregor Weber, and Arthur Wheelock. I have benefitted greatly from the abundant number of enthusiastic and supportive specialists among my colleagues at the University of Amsterdam, including Piet Bakker, Frans Grijzenhout, Hanneke Grootenboer, Rozemarijn Landsman, and Judith Noorman.

Last but most of all, for their unstinting support on the home front, I would like to express my utmost appreciation and admiration for my wife, Ilona van Tuinen, who kindly commented on all the text at various stages, and for our daughter, Mathilde, whose patience with my time devoted to this project, along with her mother's, has been quite remarkable. I cannot thank them enough.

ROBERT FUCCI

INTRODUCTION

L OVE LETTERS PROMISE an unmasking of emotion, whether of longing, desire, or even injury. Whatever the contents, they are reflective of a sustained conversation across time and space in which privacy is paramount. The written word requires a greater focus on the precision of expression than the spoken word, even though the fate of the resulting message inherently lacks certainty when it comes to delivery, the unobservable impact, and the occasionally unbearable wait for a reply. It is a range of emotions that many of us can relate to today, whether behind our computers or on our phones, moments created through the exchange of written words that mark the passage of sometimes dramatic or even life-altering junctures in friendships, family, work, or indeed love.

For Johannes Vermeer (1632–1675) and his contemporaries, the act of writing and receiving letters was a theme worthy of painting because the inner lives of their subjects could be given visual expression; that is, they were drawn to this subject precisely because the complex emotions involved demanded artistry of the highest order. Outcomes could remain unclear, and all the more so since the goal was not to explain but to offer viewers touchstones for reflection, encased in a wealth of brilliant brushstrokes. This does not mean that these works are empty of meaning. Vermeer's letter-themed paintings all focus on women. Ultimately, he advocates, in a profound way, for a sympathetic view of what was (especially at the time) an intensely private aspect of women's lives.

Six of Vermeer's paintings take reading, writing, or receiving letters as their subject. This is a significant portion of his surviving oeuvre, which numbers only around thirty-seven works.

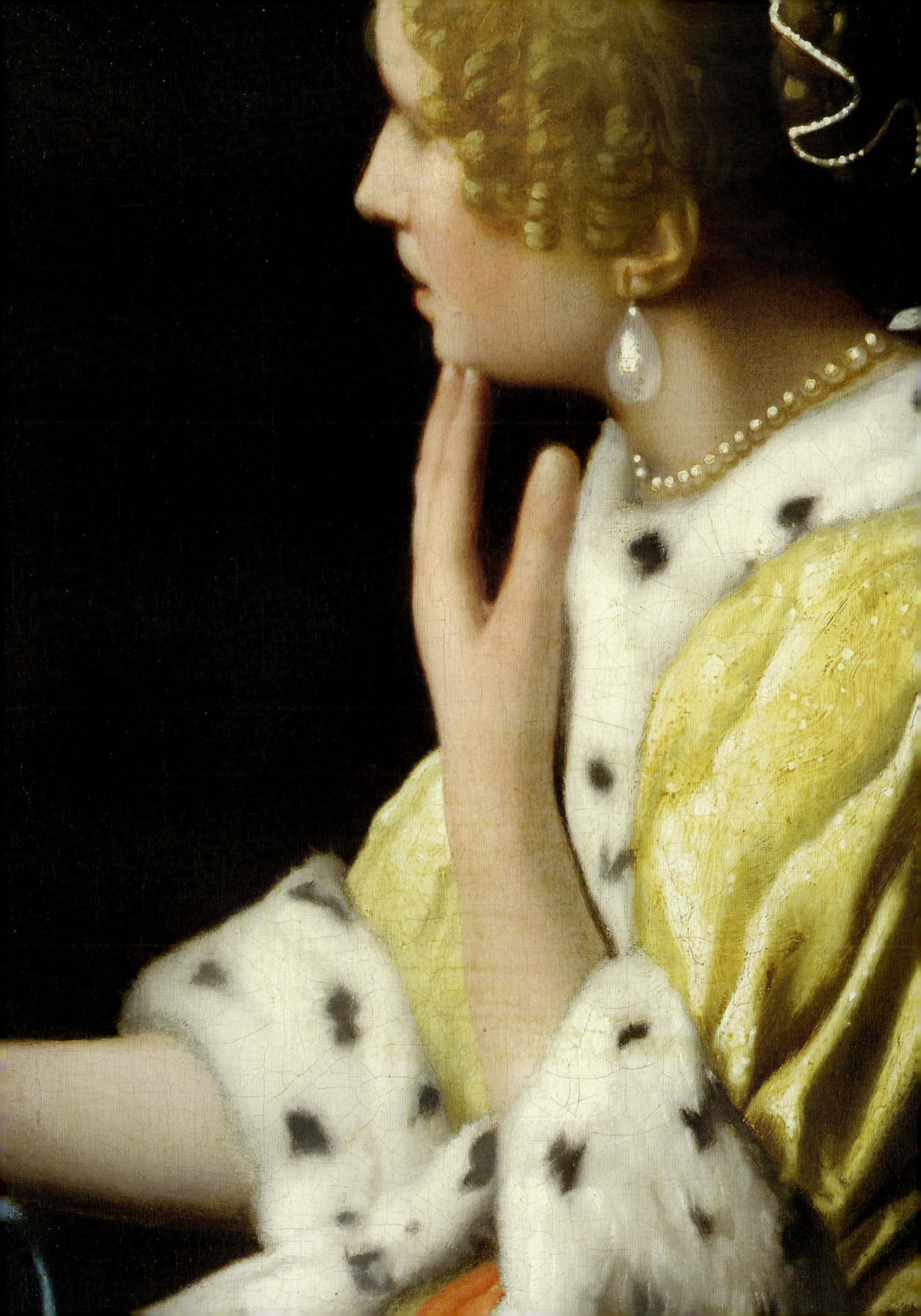

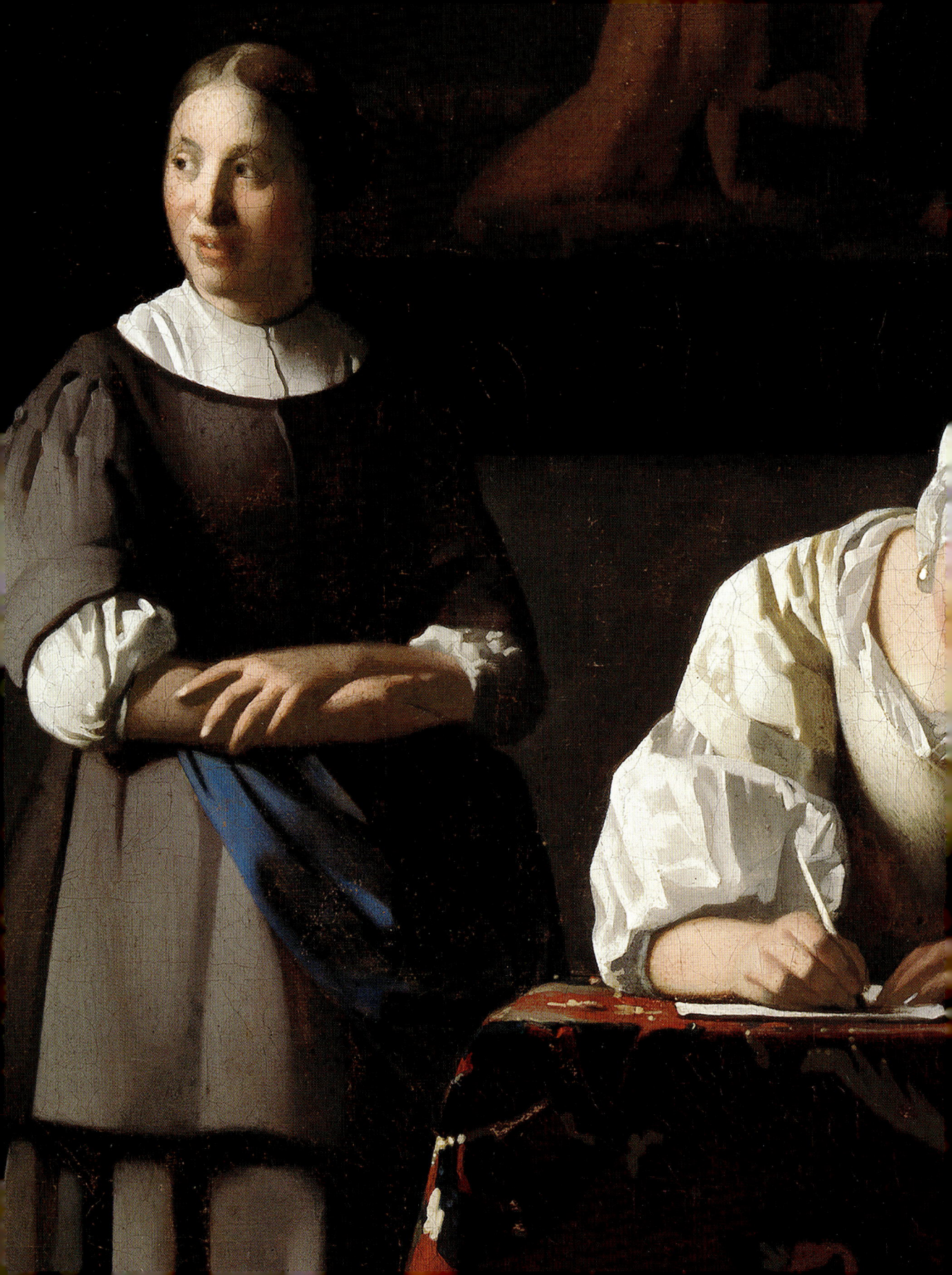

Three of these, likely painted earlier in his career, take solitary women as their subject. Our main focus, however, is the group of three paintings that bring a maidservant into the scene as a near-equal protagonist, at least in visual form: *Mistress and Maid*, *The Love Letter*, and *Woman Writing a Letter with Her Maid*. Of course, the social status of the maidservant would not have been equal to that of the young woman, or *juffrouw* (lady); but in all three paintings, the two figures appear to be on familiar terms. Vermeer gained much by introducing this secondary figure. The maid provides narrative motion, serving as the customary go-between for the delivery and receipt of letters. In Vermeer's hands, however, she also serves as a subtle foil, her interaction with the *juffrouw* yielding greater interpretive space for the emotions at play.

In his three paintings of the subject, Vermeer took different approaches to exploring this interaction. In *Mistress and Maid* (cat. 1), the *juffrouw* looks up from her writing with an expression of concerned attention, fingers lightly touching her chin as the maid comes in to deliver a letter and imparts verbally (we can assume since her mouth is slightly open) some additional intelligence. The scale is relatively large for a painting by Vermeer in his mature years, and it brings the viewer close to the figures from a low viewpoint. This effect monumentalizes the scene, building a moment arranged around anticipation and uncertainty. By contrast, *The Love Letter* (cat. 2), likely made a few years later, offers subtle differences in interaction and a profound difference in visual approach. The young woman is again interrupted, this time while practicing her stringed instrument (a cittern). The concern on her face is more apparent to the viewer since she is not facing away. The maid offers a clearly visible smile, conveying an attitude that is at odds with the discomfort of the young woman. The scale of the painting is much smaller and the brushstrokes tighter. More significantly, the viewer now plays an active role in the image as someone spying on the scene from the next room. For *Woman Writing a Letter with Her Maid* (cat. 3), perhaps the latest of the three, Vermeer moved away from a direct interaction between the figures. Here the maid waits patiently while the *juffrouw* writes, deep in her work and with intense mental and emotional concentration.

CHAPTER 1

Letters

THE POPULARITY OF LOVE LETTERS as a central theme in Dutch art reached its height from the late 1650s to the early 1670s, a period that coincides with Vermeer's six treatments of the subject.[1] Falling broadly into a category called high-life genre painting, they feature contemporary figures in richly appointed settings, often painted with great precision and attention to detail.[2] The few extant sales records demonstrate that it was a popular and occasionally quite profitable genre, despite the fact that paintings of historical, biblical, or mythological subjects ("history painting") were traditionally more highly valued among artists and collectors.[3] None of the six Vermeer paintings is dated, and only a few by his contemporaries are, which makes it difficult to frame a chronological development of the subject in Dutch art in these years. Significant for all these painters, however, was the interchange of artistic ideas. They clearly took an interest in each other's pictorial innovations, and they quite freely produced variations on each other's themes.[4]

Once described by a visitor to his studio as an "excellent" and "celebrated" painter,[5] Vermeer was a well-known and respected artist. On occasion, he served as head of the painters' guild. As a connoisseur, he was once called upon for his opinion on the authenticity of an expensive group of Italian Renaissance paintings being offered for sale in The Hague. There is also evidence that as a side business he bought and sold paintings by others. Both business and personal matters in Vermeer's life demanded a fair degree of travel, made all the easier by the recently developed intercity canal boat service (the *trekschuit*). This would have furthered his opportunities to see

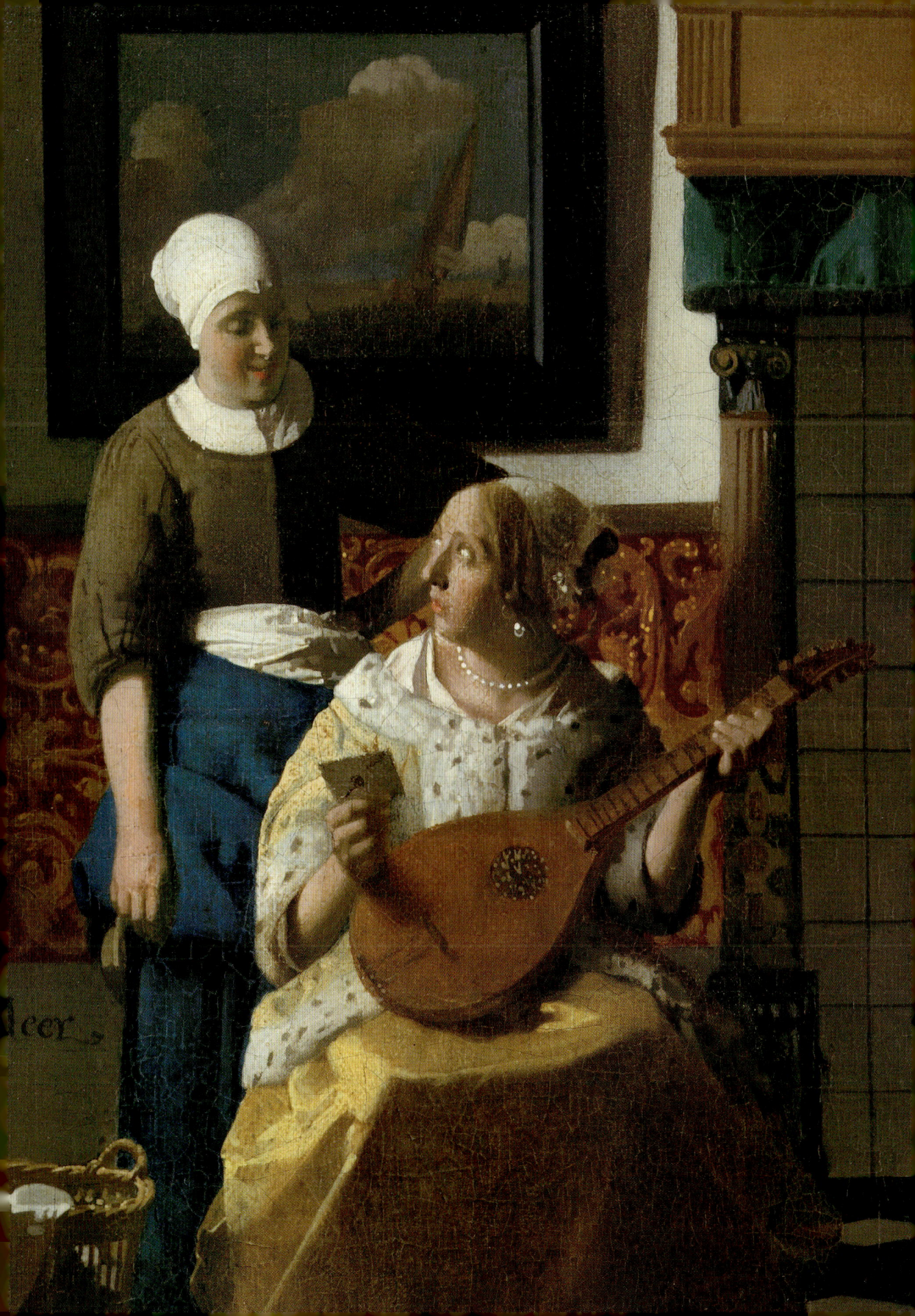

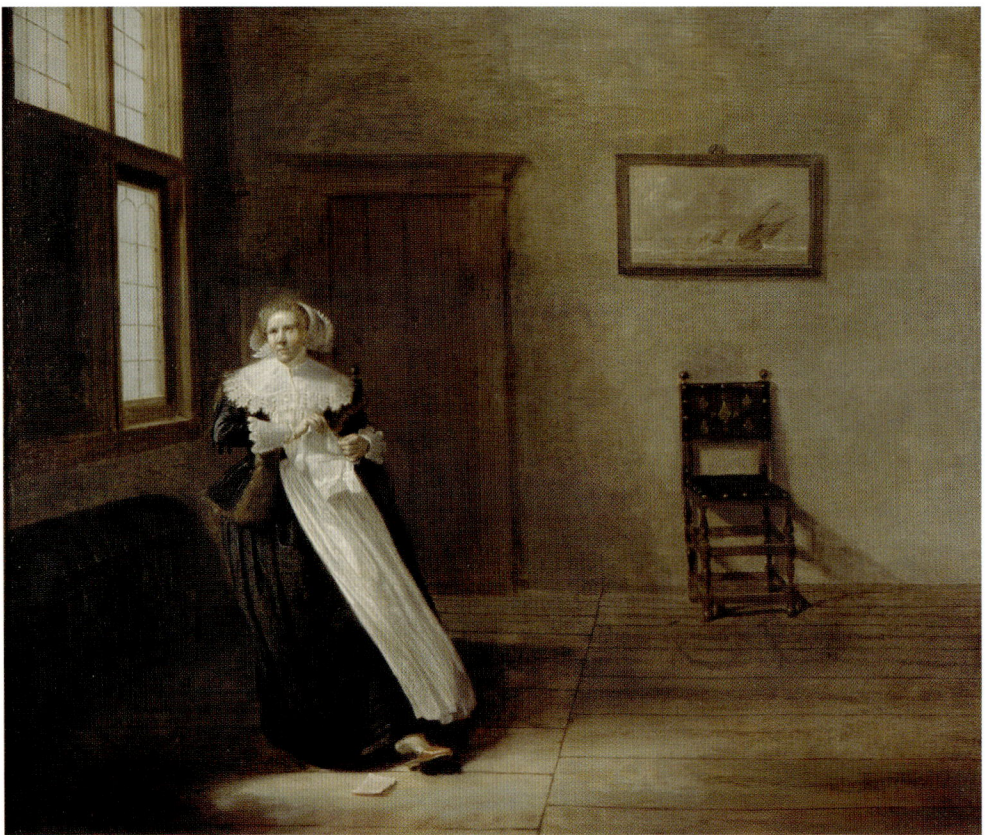

works by other artists, to discuss matters with them, and to share ideas about the possibilities of image-making in an age of rapidly changing ideals and tastes. Any vision we may have had of Vermeer working in single-minded isolation in his hometown of Delft is a myth. He appears to have been a highly engaged and collegial painter.

The acts of reading, writing, and receiving letters offered fertile and wide-ranging subjects for painters to explore and for their publics to enjoy. Much of their appeal is the access they provide to private moments about which a great deal can be implied without being explicitly stated. Subtlety frequently characterizes treatments of this subject and is one of the hallmarks of seventeenth-century letter-themed paintings by Dutch artists. Among the few surviving precedents from earlier in the century are two paintings by Dirck Hals (1591–1656), brother of the famous Frans, signed and dated 1631 and 1633, respectively, showing a full-length woman with a letter in her hand (figs. 1, 2).[6] In the former, she appears to be wringing or tearing the letter, her mood reflected by the stormy seas in the painting hanging on the wall in the background, while in the latter, the smiling woman is perfectly in accord with the fair-weather seascape behind her. Hals's intent with the seascapes is to provide a direct and perhaps even comic allusion to his subjects' moods. Amatory literature from the time often compared the changing fortunes of

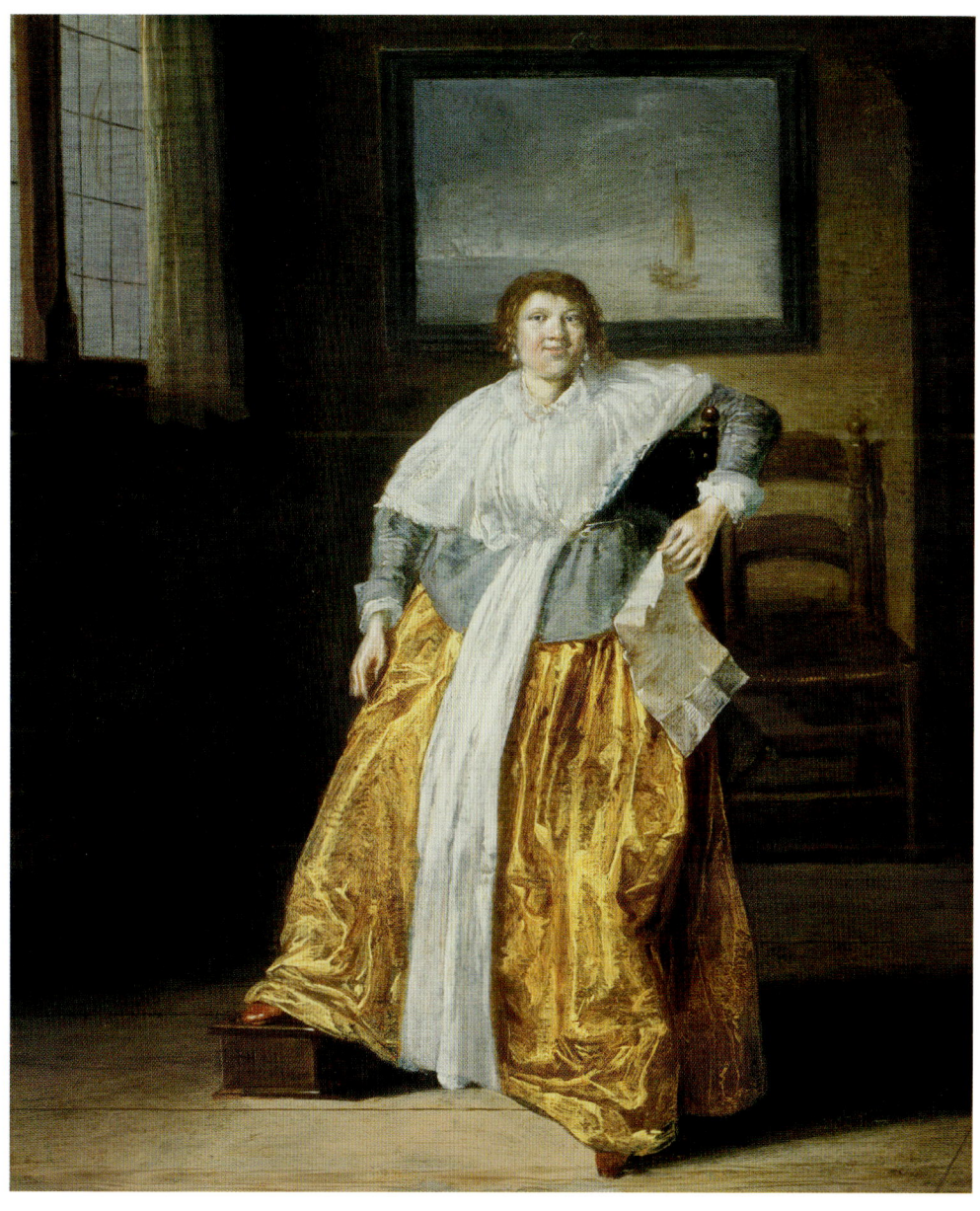

FIG. 1

Dirck Hals

Woman Tearing up a Letter, 1631

Oil on panel, 17¾ × 21⅝ in. (45 × 55 cm)

Landesmuseum, Mainz

FIG. 2

Dirck Hals

Seated Woman with a Letter, 1633

Oil on panel, 13⁵⁄₁₆ × 11¼ in. (33.8 × 28.6 cm)

Philadelphia Museum of Art

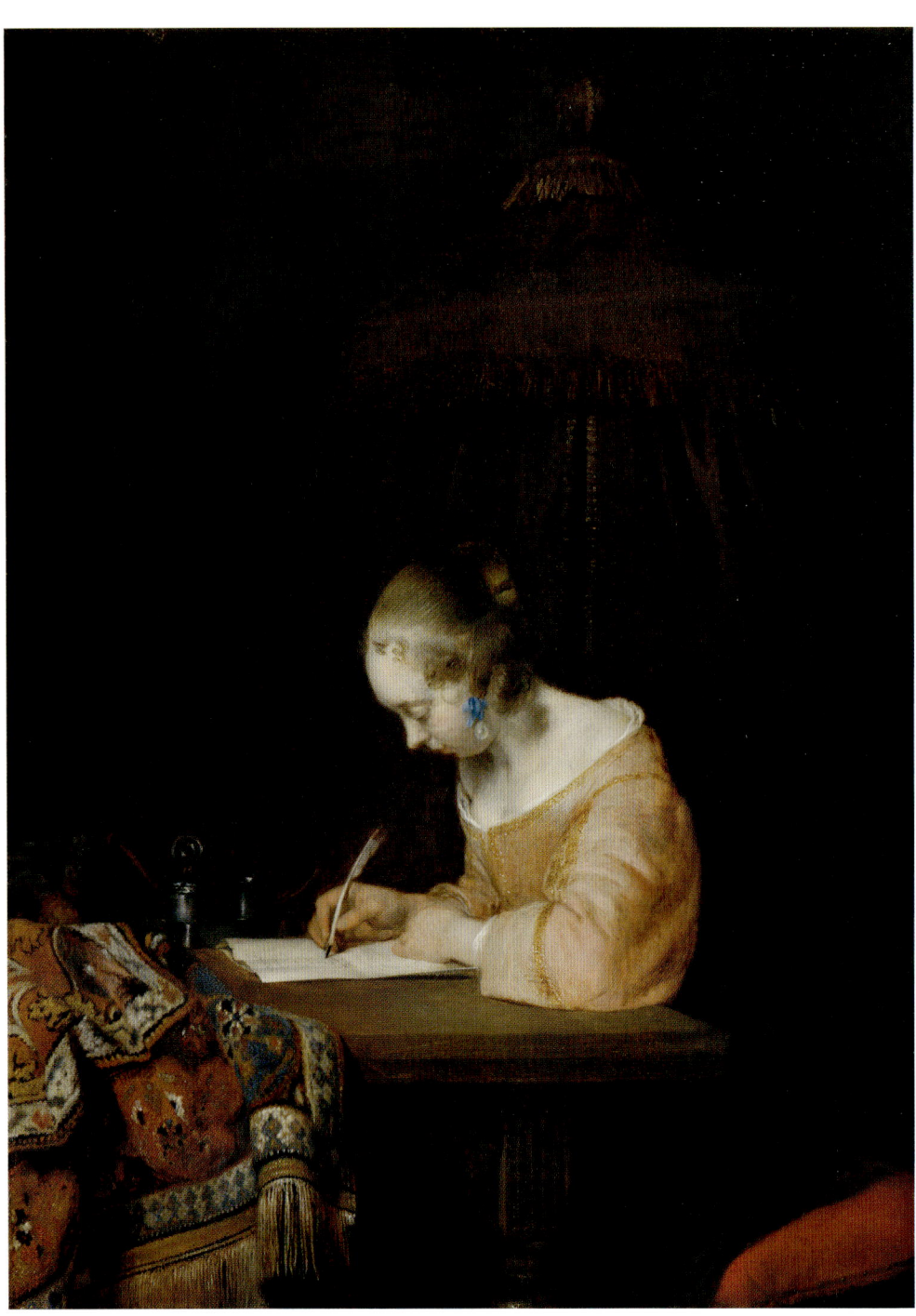

love with the changing winds at sea.[7] There is also a congruence with the historical importance of maritime travel for the seafaring nation and the proportionally high number of men away at sea who would maintain contact through letters. While the picture-within-a-picture concept seems straightforward in these cases, such an approach would have a long afterlife. Years later, the use of seascapes in backgrounds would be taken up by Vermeer and his contemporaries for many of their own love-themed paintings, such as *The Love Letter* (cat. 2).[8]

A new and more sustained interest in letter-themed paintings arose during Vermeer's generation, one of the earliest examples of which is the *Woman Writing a Letter*, by Gerard ter Borch (1617–1681) (fig. 3).[9] The well-dressed and elaborately coiffed young woman has pushed aside the carpet covering the table in order to gain a better writing surface. Next to her is one of the many examples of a fashionable and expensive silver tray with inkpot and sander (sometimes with a third pot for holding quills) found in so many paintings with letter-writing subjects. No full-size examples of these silver inkstands apparently survive, though one miniature version from the seventeenth century—perhaps intended for a doll's set or made as a collectible—can be found in the Rijksmuseum (fig. 4).[10] In Ter Borch's painting, the effective rendering of the woman's quiet yet intense focus appears to have been the main artistic concern. Notably, the letter has already been written and folded, possibly indicating that she is making a last-minute change to the text. Such details could have been designed to serve as points of discussion among observant viewers.

One might question whether she is actually writing a love letter, but the boudoir setting and the painting's relationship to other courtship-themed works by Ter Borch and others seem to make that a safe assumption. In this case, Ter Borch used his favorite model, his younger

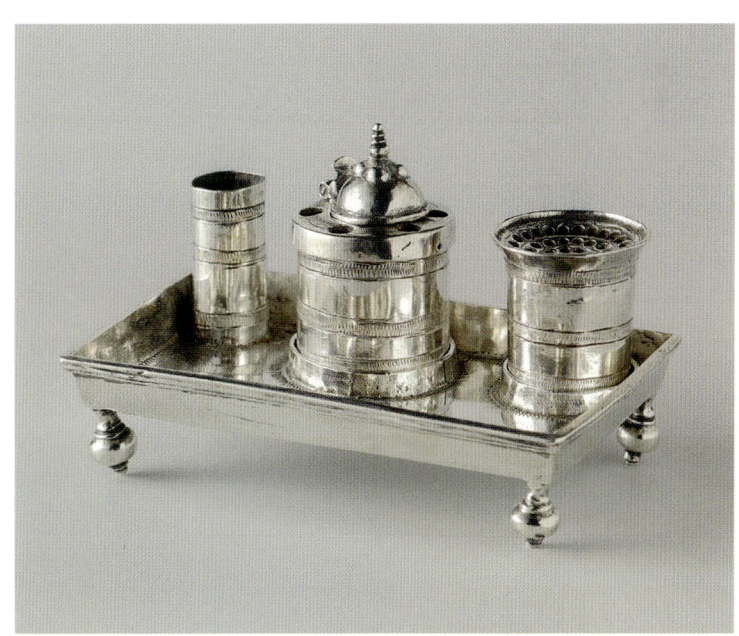

FIG. 3
Gerard ter Borch
Woman Writing a Letter,
ca. 1655
Oil on panel, 15 1/16 × 11 in.
(38.3 × 27.9 cm)
Mauritshuis, The Hague

FIG. 4
Wessel Jansen
Inkstand, late 17th century
Silver, 3 1/8 × 2 × 1 13/16 in.
(8 × 5 × 4.6 cm)
Rijksmuseum, Amsterdam

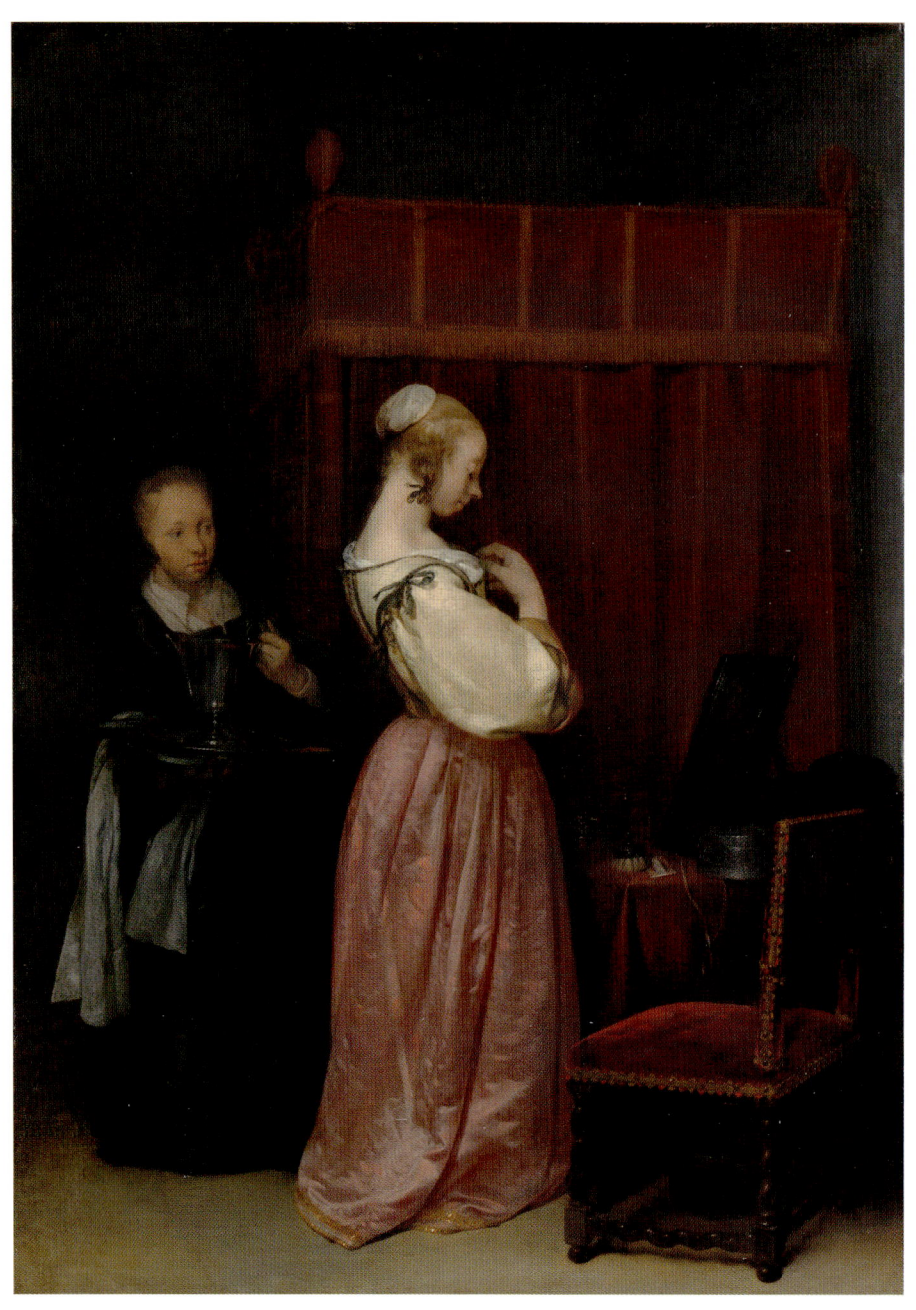

FIG. 5
Gerard ter Borch
A Young Woman at Her Toilet with a Maid, ca. 1650–51
Oil on panel, 18¾ × 13⅝ in. (47.6 × 34.6 cm)
The Metropolitan Museum of Art, New York

half-sister, Gesina ter Borch (1631–1690), herself a painter and watercolorist.[11] Gesina features in a number of his other genre scenes showing women with letters, occupied with music, or preparing themselves in front of a mirror, such as *A Young Woman at Her Toilet with a Maid* (fig. 5).[12] Given that corresponding themes of love, music, and vanity are hallmarks of both their oeuvres, it comes as no surprise that an archival document reveals that Gerard ter Borch and Vermeer knew each other personally, although the exact nature of their relationship remains unclear.[13] On April 22, 1653, Ter Borch and Vermeer served as witnesses for a deposition related to an "act of surety" signed in Delft. Notably, Vermeer had married two days previously, and it is tempting to posit that Ter Borch, who would soon settle in Deventer, had come to Delft specifically to celebrate Vermeer's nuptials. The document has led to conjecture that Ter Borch could have been Vermeer's teacher, the identification of whom has long been a matter of debate.[14] One of the problems with Ter Borch's candidacy is that Vermeer's early works (those made between 1653 and 1657) betray no signs of Ter Borch's tutelage, though their artistic approaches would later converge in terms of style and subject matter.

Vermeer's Letter Readers

Vermeer's artistic transformation came around 1657, when he moved away from religious, mythological, and conventional genre subjects and began to try his hand at more ambiguous love- or courtship-themed works.[15] One of the earliest of these is the *Girl Reading a Letter at an Open Window*, which is generally thought to date to about 1657–58 (fig. 6).[16] Around the same time, he also produced the Frick's *Officer and Laughing Girl* (fig. 7), showing a similar young woman who also wears a yellow bodice with black stripes.[17] In *Girl Reading a Letter at an Open Window*, Vermeer depicts a private, unguarded moment of reading. From the mood alone, one can assume that the letter contains deeply personal content. The fact that the paper is crumpled suggests that it has already been read several times. The young woman's image in the glass window reflects (literally and figuratively) the internalization of her emotions, distinct yet blurred, brought forth by the words she absorbs. The large painting of Cupid in the background was recently revealed by a major restoration project. It had previously been covered by a layer of white paint, famously thought to have indicated Vermeer's change of mind when the Cupid painting underneath was discovered with X-rays more than fifty years ago; but recent analysis reveals that a later (probably eighteenth-century) hand covered up the figure.[18] Cupid, of course, serves to make the love-letter theme explicit, one of Vermeer's most direct doublings using the picture-within-a-picture device. Even so, with the inclusion of masks on the ground, one of which Cupid tramples, he allows a range of interpretive nuances. Such imagery associating love with the unmasking of emotions that accompany desire can also be found in contemporary Dutch emblem books.[19]

Several years later, around 1663, Vermeer made his second image of a letter reader, the *Woman in Blue Reading a Letter* (fig. 8).[20] The painting is considerably smaller but similar in composition and concept; in it, we act as privileged viewers who observe, from a slightly remote position, the woman's internal absorption in the text. In contrast to *Girl Reading a Letter at an*

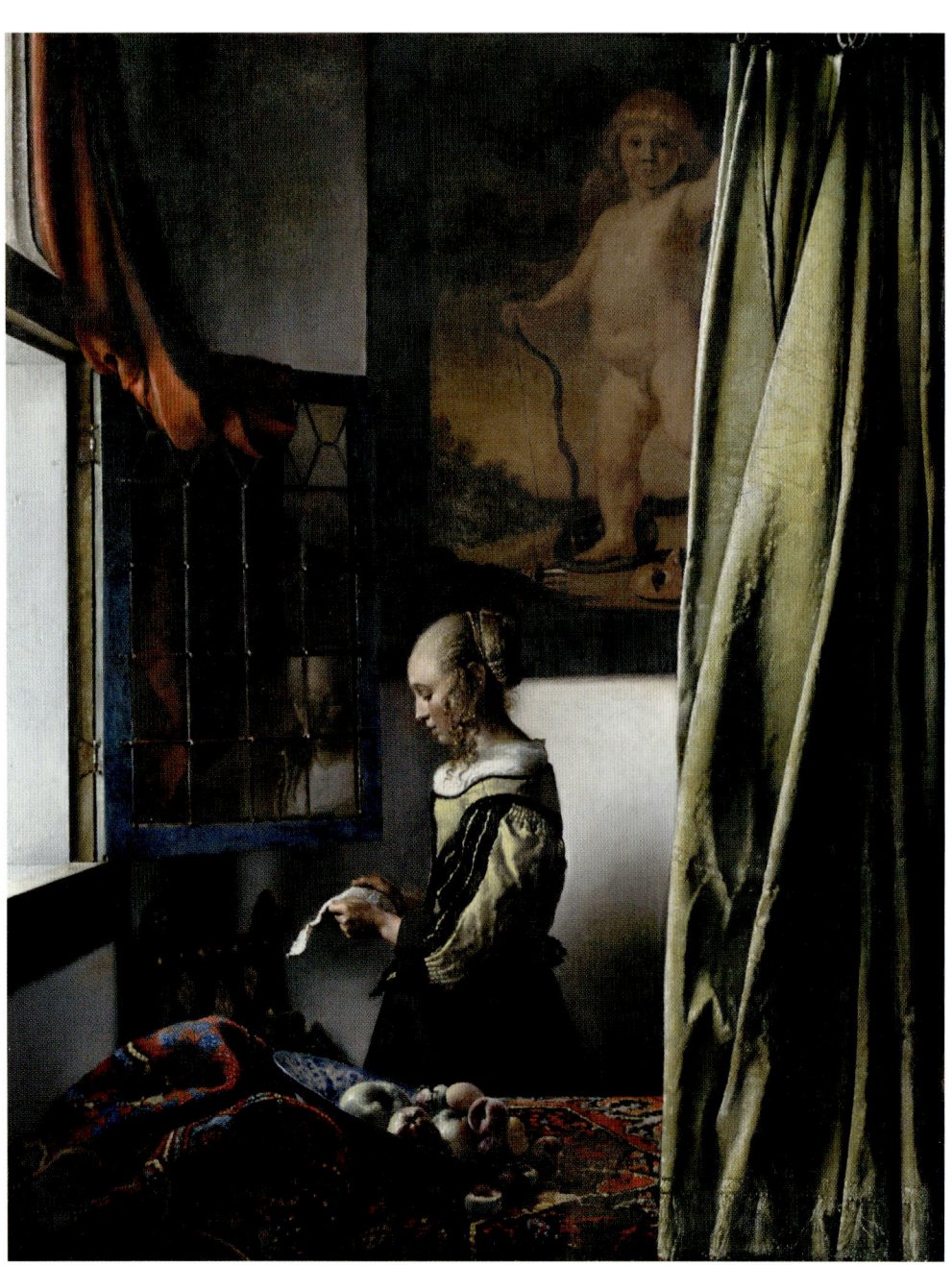

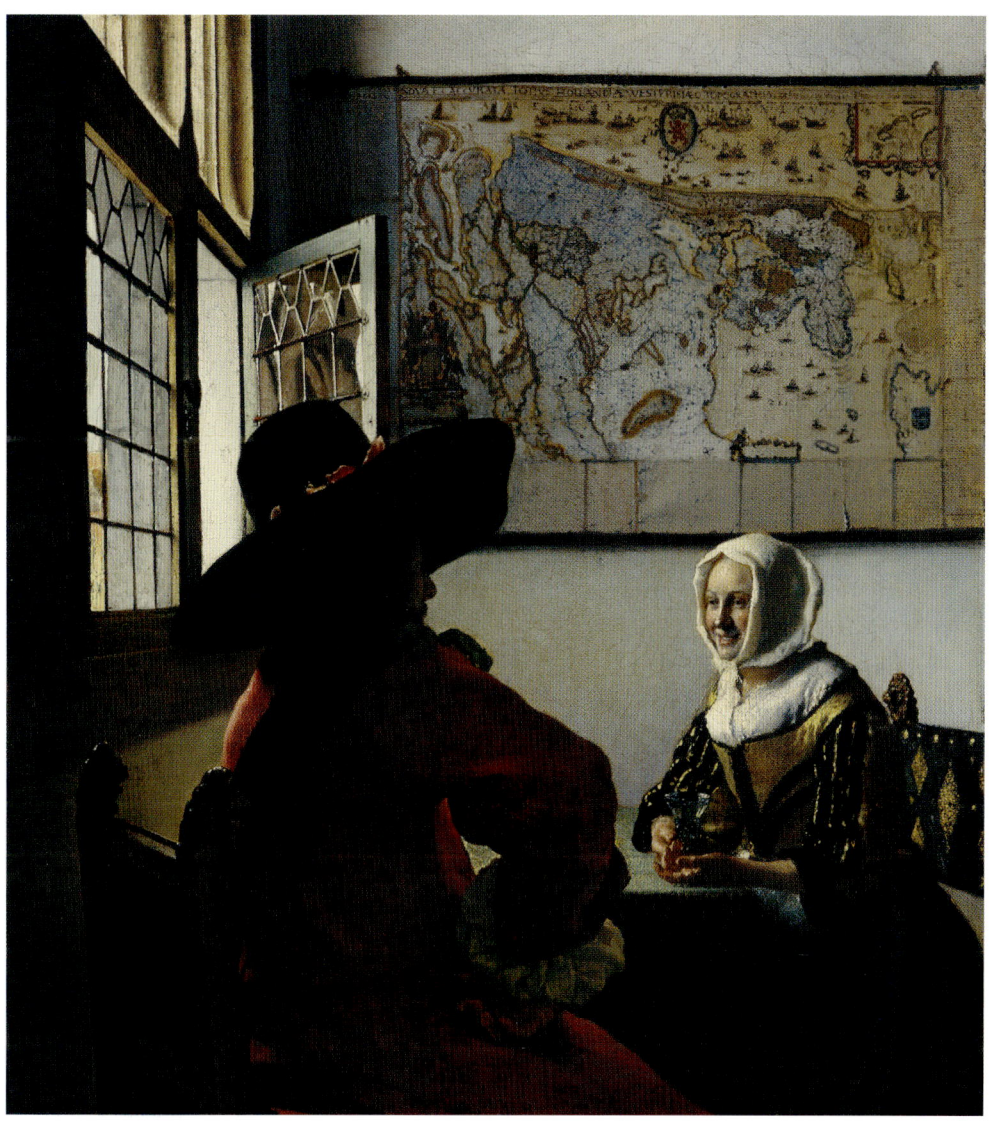

FIG. 6
Johannes Vermeer
Girl Reading a Letter at an Open Window, ca. 1657–58
Oil on canvas, 32¹¹⁄₁₆ × 25⅜ in. (83 × 64.5 cm)
Gemäldegalerie Alte Meister,
Staatliche Kunstsammlungen, Dresden

FIG. 7
Johannes Vermeer
Officer and Laughing Girl, ca. 1657–58
Oil on canvas, 19⅞ × 18⅛ in. (50.5 × 46 cm)
The Frick Collection, New York

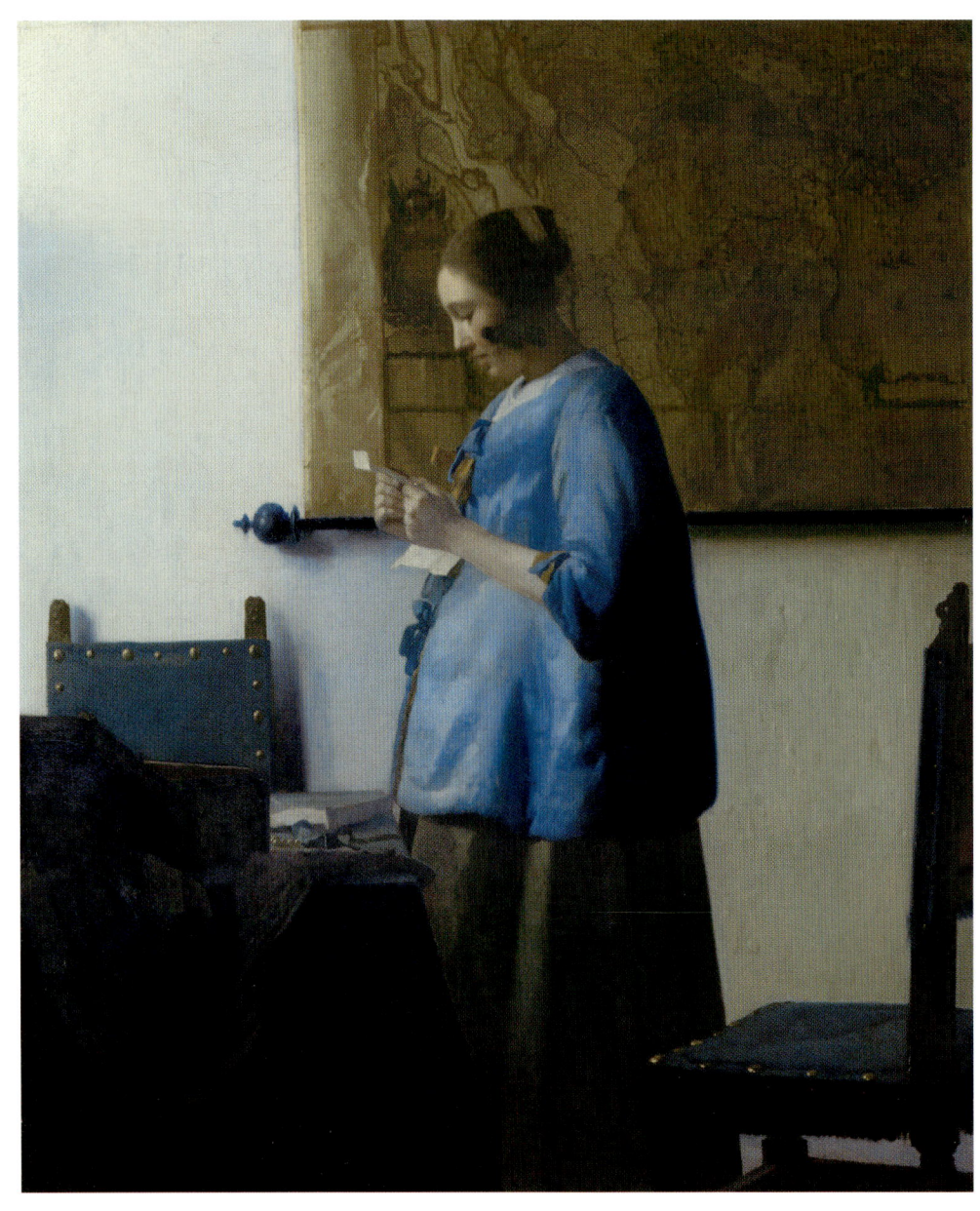

FIG. 8
Johannes Vermeer
Woman in Blue Reading a Letter, ca. 1662–64
Oil on canvas, 18⁵⁄₁₆ × 15⅜ in. (46.5 × 39 cm)
Rijksmuseum, Amsterdam

Open Window, Vermeer subtly suggests that she is reading the letter for the first time. The paper edges are crisp, and a second sheet lies on the table, partially covering the string of pearls that she has not yet donned, as if the letter had been brought to her while she was preparing herself for the day.[21] The map on the wall behind her could suggest that the letter has come from afar, but there are no obvious clues about the nature of the missive. A long-standing matter of debate is whether the woman is pregnant.[22] Some scholars find pregnancy incongruous for a genre painting of this type, while others see it as stating the obvious. If we accept that Vermeer intended to depict an expectant mother reading a letter, the image gains greater poignancy. It could still be seen as an amatory subject, perhaps the exchange of letters between husband and wife. It seems unlikely that Vermeer would have considered marriage or betrothal as impediments to the development of an artistic theme around love and longing.

Women of Letters

In the seventeenth century, the Dutch enjoyed one of the highest literacy rates in Europe, a fact connected to the mercantile structure of Dutch society, which necessarily made widespread use of the written word. Other factors included an expansive printing and publishing culture and an educational system that benefited from economic prosperity. Exact numbers are difficult to come by, but one study of Amsterdam wedding records shows that 75 percent of men and 40 percent of women could sign their names.[23] Being able to sign your name and to compose messages are of course two different things. Even more fundamental to our understanding of early modern literacy is the distinction between reading and writing as two different skills, with writing taught to children a few years later than reading. Although such proficiencies can be difficult to measure, maids and other servants were more likely to be able to read, at least to some degree, than to write. Such rates did not remain static since literacy increased considerably throughout the century.

Reading aloud was a common practical necessity to impart messages to the illiterate, and some painters adopted the act of listening as a subject. In Ludolf de Jongh's *Message* (fig. 9), the inhabitants of a modest structure (perhaps an inn) give their full attention to a messenger reading a letter or the news.[24] Pieter de Hooch, who was De Jongh's student, brought the theme of listening into wealthier environs in his *Man Reading a Letter to a Woman* (fig. 10).[25] The fashionably dressed woman in this work may have been perfectly capable of reading, but she obviously enjoys this relaxing moment of listening. Love letters in this early modern context, especially in visual culture, are notable precisely for the implication of silent and therefore private consumption, which counters a norm in which the written word was often shared publicly.

Literacy can be assumed for women in the upper echelons of society, such as those depicted in Vermeer's paintings. They were also likely to be fluent in French, which was by far the most popular second language at the time. For these women, and much of the upper middle class generally, writing would have been a vital aspect of their lives, whether pursuing legal matters, communicating with family, or keeping household accounts.[26] To some degree, therefore, letters

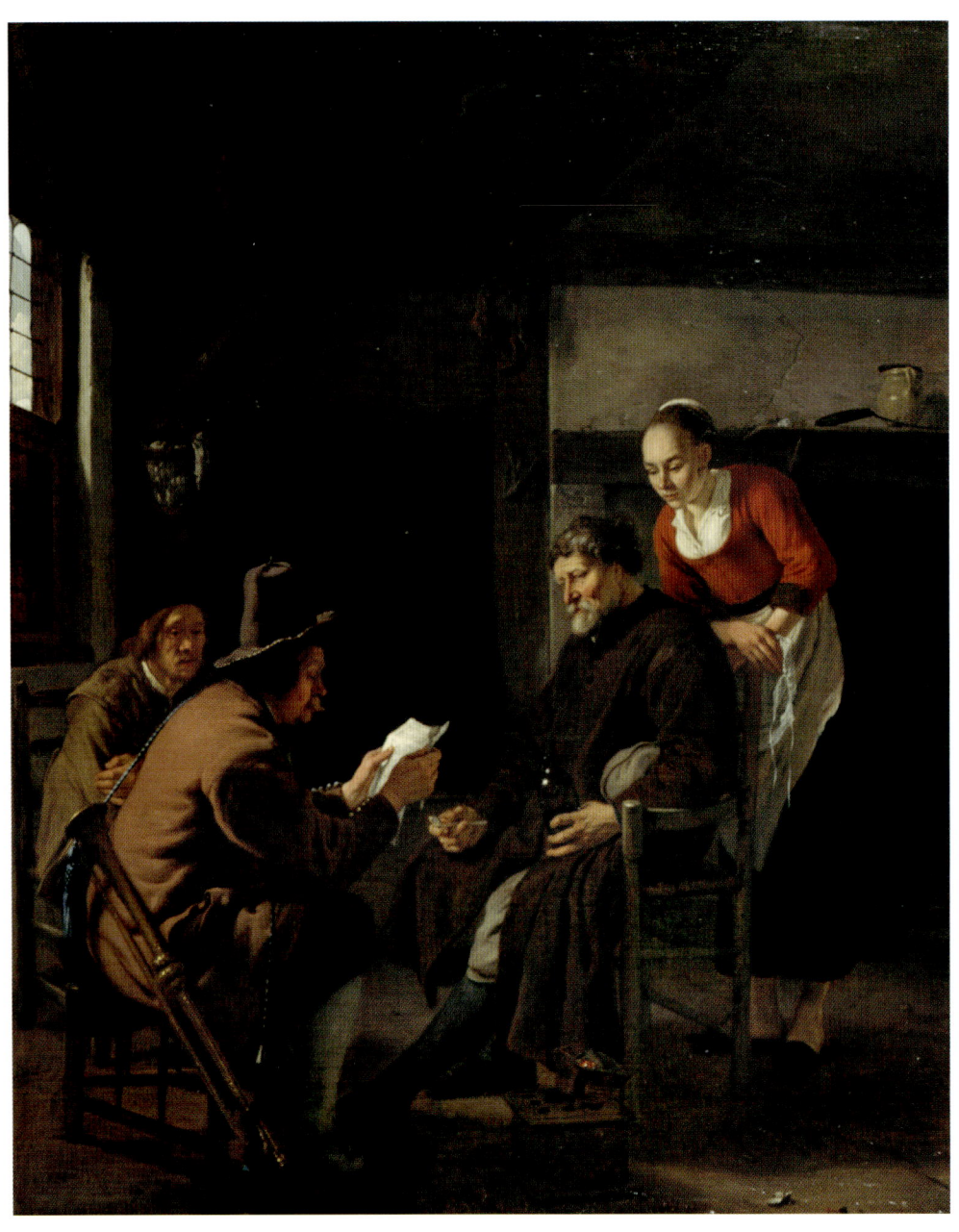

FIG. 9
Ludolf de Jongh
The Message, 1657
Oil on canvas, 25⁹⁄₁₆ × 20⅞ in. (65 × 53 cm)
Landesmuseum, Mainz

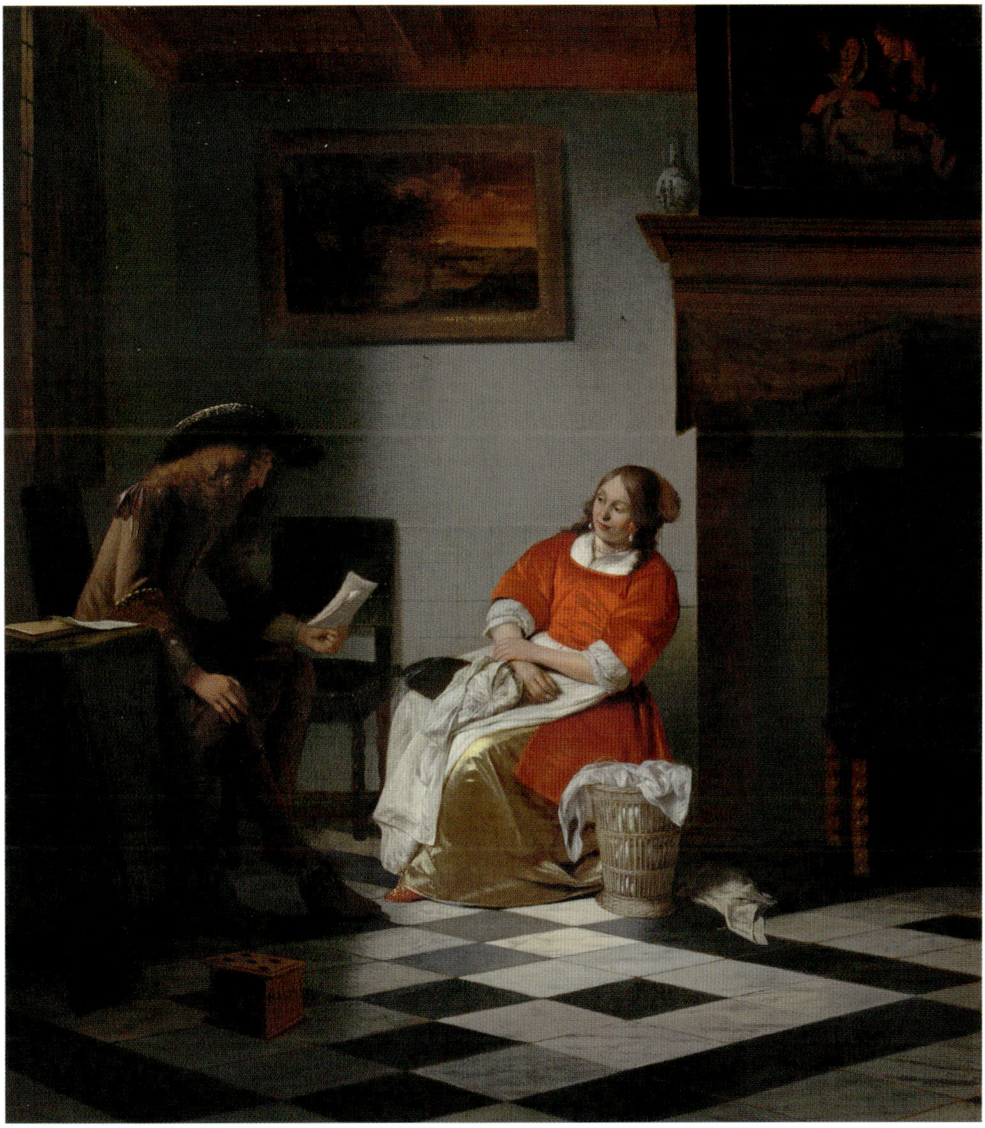

FIG. 10
Pieter de Hooch
Man Reading a Letter to a Woman, ca. 1670–74
Oil on canvas, 30⁵⁄₁₆ × 27½ in. (77 × 69.9 cm)
The Kremer Collection, Amsterdam

can be understood as a means through which women exercised agency on a daily basis. Another category of letter that has received great attention is that written by the most intellectual women of the era. Men and women across Europe shared opinions, philosophies, scientific observations, musical compositions, and verses with each other in epistolary form. Grouped today under the term Republic of Letters, this body of literature served as an early modern equivalent of literary and academic journals.[27] Many learned women were actively engaged and highly respected members of this community of scholars, poets, and musicians.

Sisters Anna Roemers Visscher (1584–1651) and Maria Tesselschade Visscher (1594–1649), famed figures from the early part of the century, knew Greek and Latin, among other languages, and practiced arts such as glass engraving and poetry. They corresponded and mixed socially with other leading lights, including P. C. Hooft (1581–1647), the most famous Dutch poet and playwright of the day, whom they would visit on occasion at the castle in Muiden, just outside of Amsterdam, where he served as bailiff. The so-called Muiderkring (the "Muiden Circle")—the name given to the group of writers and musicians that Hooft regularly welcomed at the castle—was later commemorated somewhat mythically as salon-like gatherings of literary men and women, though their visits were actually less formal.[28] The most famous learned Dutch woman of the century was Anna Maria van Schurman (1607–1678), "the Star of Utrecht," who became the first European woman to receive a university education.[29] Van Schurman commanded an astonishing array of languages (at least a dozen, some non-European) and deeply impressed her contemporaries with her wide-ranging erudition and artistic abilities.

Constantijn Huygens (1596–1687), courtier and secretary to the ruling Princes of Orange, was by profession and personal interest a prolific letter writer. He wrote an estimated one hundred thousand letters, out of which more than ten thousand survive. About 20 percent of them are exchanges with female correspondents.[30] Many of these are to members of the ruling classes and are political in nature, but a large number are also to and from women in the Republic of Letters, including twenty-six to and from Van Schurman. The literacy of women and their degree of literary engagement, however, should not be overstated. Latin schools, which offered the traditional path to a university education, were still closed to females. Only women from families with an interest in, and the means for, educating them were likely to become poets or scholars. Nevertheless, Arnold Houbraken, in his collection of biographies of Dutch artists published in 1718–21, compared women painters to the many women writers of the seventeenth century who had "sharpened their brains on language studies and other worthy scholarly pursuits" and had "chosen wisdom over fleeting treasures."[31]

In this context, one might ask if the subject in Vermeer's *Lady Writing* (fig. 11) might be an actual writer whom Vermeer portrayed at work rather than a model serving the purposes of a genre image.[32] Her direct engagement with the viewer and her distinctly rendered features certainly impart the sense of a portrait. Gabriel Metsu painted a similar image of a woman, this time with her quill upraised as if she had just dipped it in the inkwell and was interrupted by our sudden presence (fig. 12).[33] The sitter in Metsu's painting does not resemble his wife, whom he often used as a model, so she must be someone else. Secure likenesses of Vermeer's wife and relations are unknown, so any attempt to identify the figure in this or any other painting by Vermeer as a daughter or family member is speculative.[34]

A Lady Writing is Vermeer's only painting of a solitary figure in the act of writing. We should not exclude the possibility that Vermeer intended it to be a love-letter painting, even if he portrayed a specific sitter rather than a generalized model. The painting in the background offers little in terms of interpretive possibility since it appears to be a still life with musical instruments, though of course playing music features in many of Vermeer's love- or courtship-themed paintings.[35] The gaze and expression of the subject could be read as having amatory overtones, which would not only be in keeping with Vermeer's other letter subjects but would also be highly innovative in approach. We would no longer be silent witnesses to the emotions playing out on the page but active participants and indeed recipients of those gestures. Metsu's *Elegant Lady Writing at Her Desk* bears no date but was probably made around the same time. This was also the period in which Vermeer began incorporating a maidservant into his letter-themed paintings, the earliest of which is the Frick's *Mistress and Maid* (cat. 1). Though much larger, the Frick painting bears several marked stylistic and compositional correspondences that link it with *A Lady Writing*, such as the nearly identical pose of the seated young woman, her fur-trimmed yellow mantle, and the blue tablecloth.

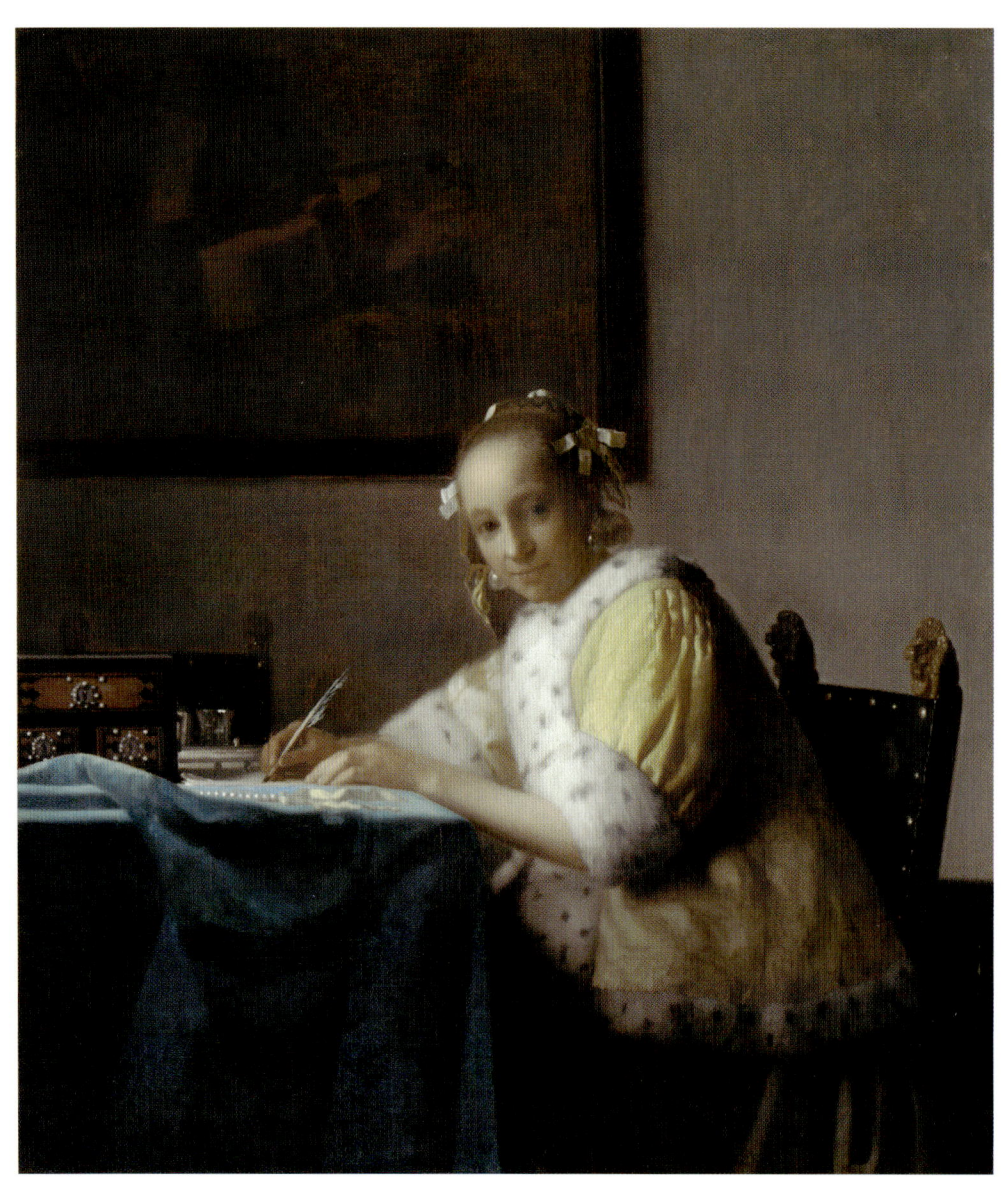

FIG. 11

Johannes Vermeer

A Lady Writing, ca. 1664–67

Oil on canvas, 17¹¹⁄₁₆ × 15¹¹⁄₁₆ in. (45 × 39.9 cm)

National Gallery of Art, Washington

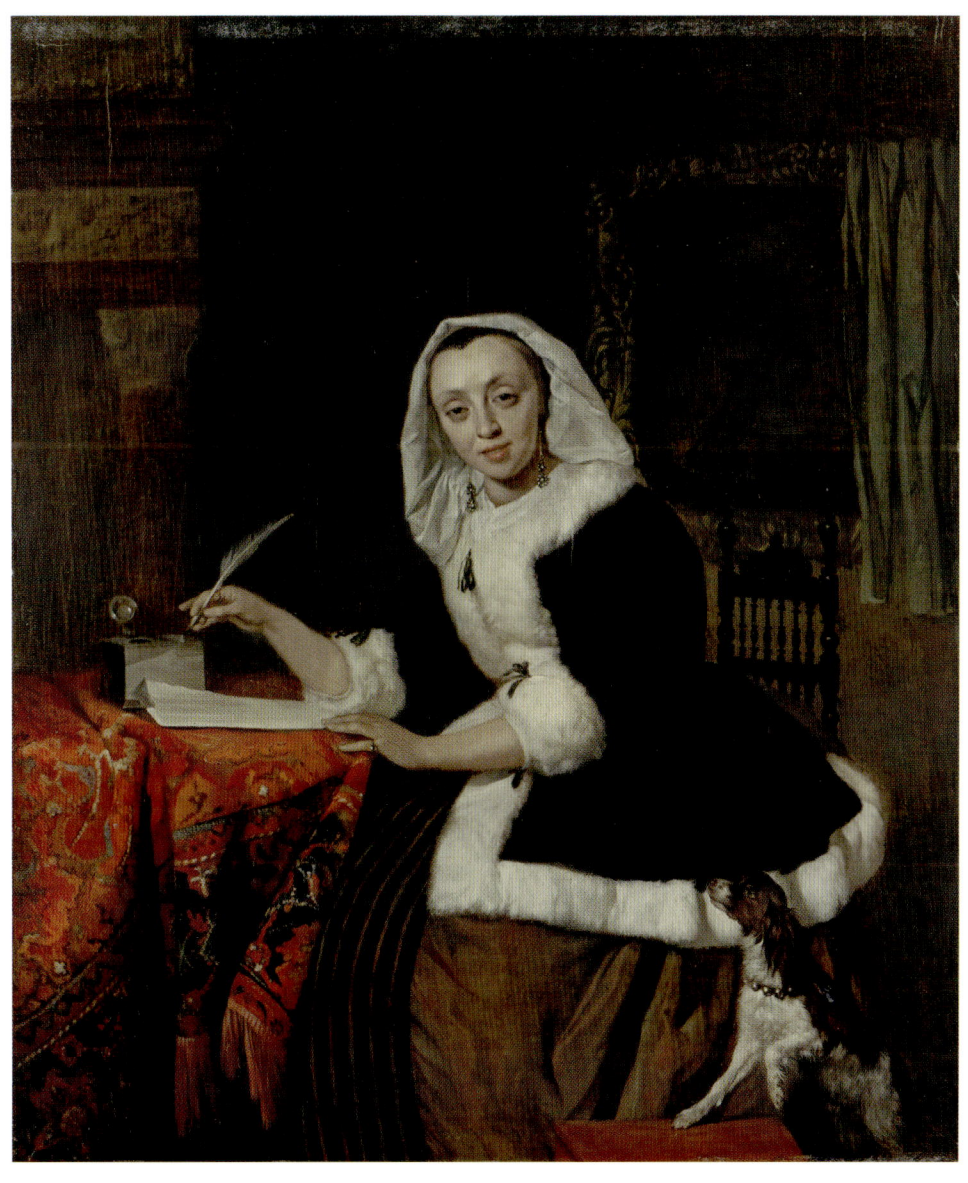

FIG. 12
Gabriel Metsu
Elegant Lady Writing at Her Desk, ca. 1662–64
Oil on panel, 15½ × 13³⁄₁₆ in.
(39.4 × 33.5 cm)
The Leiden Collection, New York

CHAPTER 2

Maids

*I*N THE MID-1660s, Vermeer began including the figure of a maid alongside the young lady of the house writing or receiving a letter. Maids served as the classic go-betweens for lovers in both literature and art (and, one can assume, in actual practice), at least when it came to local delivery. Other artists in Vermeer's orbit also adopted this pairing of figures as a means of further exploring the love-letter theme and its visual staging, though Vermeer did so with his own particular strategies. Maids had already figured prominently in a number of other types of genre paintings from the mid-seventeenth century, including in Vermeer's own.[36] Their roles ranged from affirmative expressions of an emergent and highly valued sense of domesticity to deprecatory and unambiguously patronizing images of flawed service intended, presumably, for comic effect. The realities of the life of a household servant at the time may have been quite different from the fictions of genre paintings. The latter were, by definition, one-sided and, in nearly all cases, given from a male perspective (though with some notable exceptions). Interesting in Vermeer's case is that we know the name, and even something of the character, of the maid who served in his household during the period in which he made his mistress-and-maid paintings: Tanneke Everpoel. It is entirely possible that he used Tanneke as a model for these works.

Household servants were relatively common for those who could afford them, which would have been roughly the upper 10 percent of homes in terms of income in the Dutch Republic.[37] The vast majority of these homes (except the truly wealthiest) had a single, all-purpose servant, most often a woman but sometimes a boy or man. Women were referred to as *dienstmaagd*

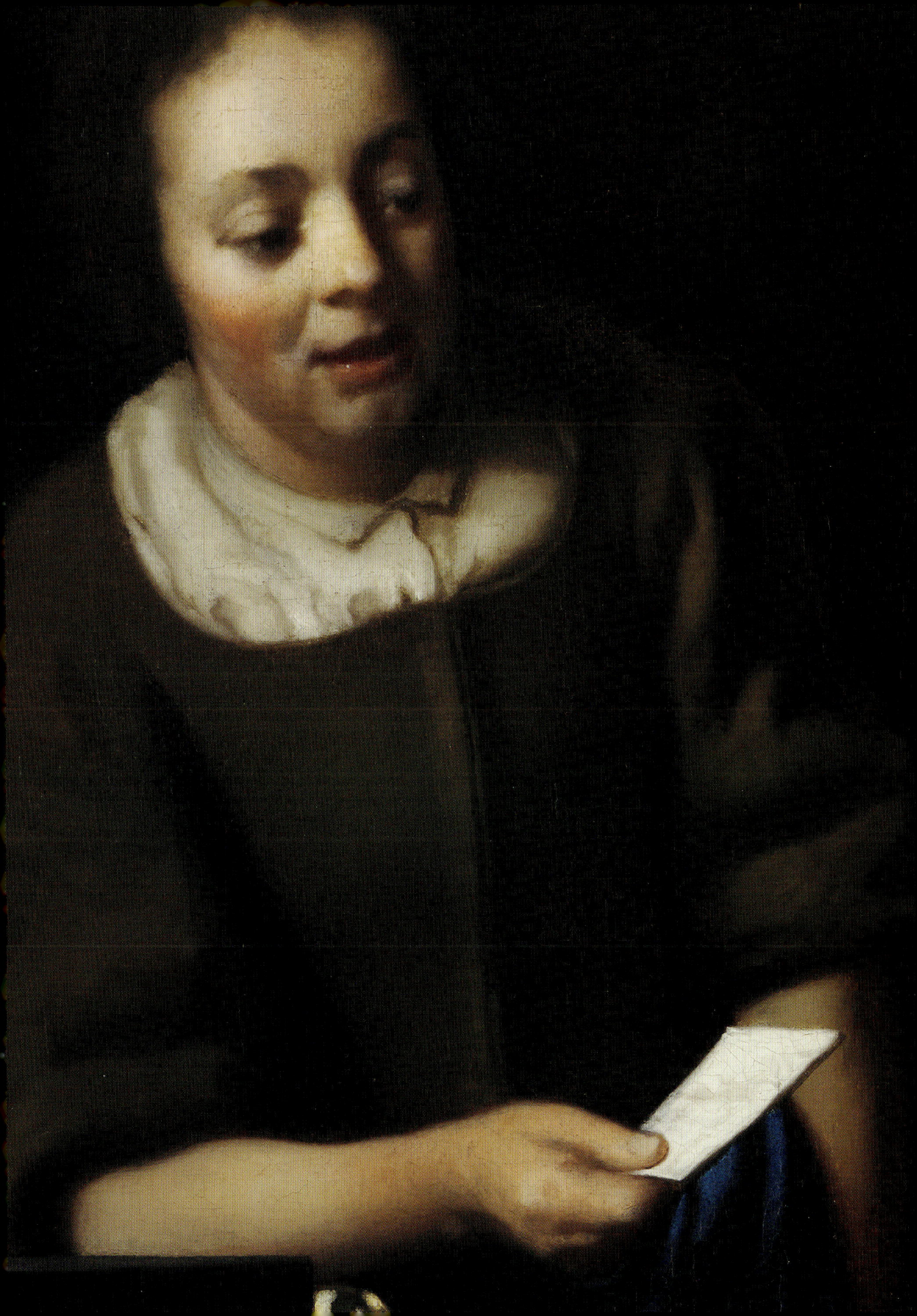

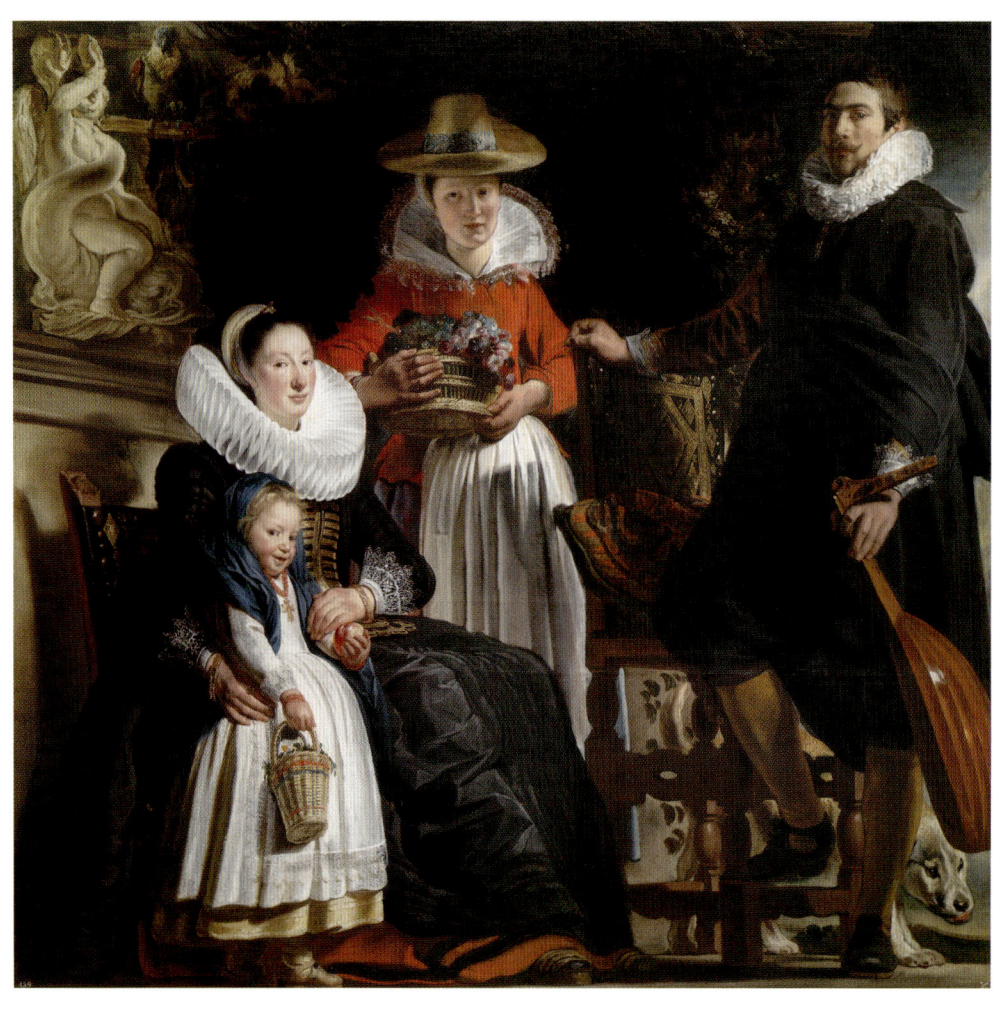

FIG. 13
Jacob Jordaens
The Painter's Family (Self-Portrait with the Artist's Wife,
Catharina van Noort, Daughter Elizabeth, and a Maid), ca. 1621–22
Oil on canvas, 71¼ × 73⅝ in. (181 × 187 cm)
Museo Nacional del Prado, Madrid

(maidservant) or *dienares* (female servant) and boys or men as *knecht* or *dienaar* (male servant). Women made up a significant majority of the domestic workforce at a time when a vast segment of the male population served in seafaring industries. There arose at the time a specialized and licensed profession of *besteedster,* a person who would supply homes with trained maids with adequate references.[38] Integration into the household was essential, as maids often lived and slept in the houses of their employers and frequently ate with the family. A testament to a maid's status in the service of Antwerp artist Jacob Jordaens (1593–1678) is that Jordaens included her in his family portrait, showing her with a basket of grapes standing between him and his wife (fig. 13). Her name is not known, but her apron and red bodice, typical for maids in Antwerp at the time, make her position clear.[39]

Servants could also play significant roles in artists' personal lives. Rembrandt had sexual relationships with two of his female servants after the early death of his wife, Saskia.[40] The first of these, with Geertje Dircx, ended tragically, with Dircx serving five years in the Spinhuis (a house of correction for women) after a "breach of promise" settlement became contentious. His subsequent relationship with Hendrickje Stoffels was long-term, lasting until her death in 1663. They had a daughter, Cornelia, who survived them (Rembrandt's only child to do so). Rembrandt never married Stoffels, which led to censure by her church in 1654 for living in sin—literally, in *hoererij* (whoredom)—with the artist, but it was a judgment they endured. A completely different type of relationship was that between the renowned still-life painter Maria van Oosterwijck (1630–1693) and her maid, Geertgen Wyntges (1636–1712). She first trained her to mix colors, no doubt to be helpful in the studio, but then also to paint. Ultimately, Wyntges painted well enough to become a self-supporting artist, a remarkable story in an era when the paths for women to train as painters were so limited.[41]

Maids and female servants played narrative roles in many subjects found in early modern painting. In biblical art, Judith slayed Holofernes with the aid of her elderly servant. Hagar was a servant before Abraham banished her to the wilderness with their son Ishmael. When Christ visited the house of Martha and Mary, Martha kept to her work in the kitchen, while Mary abandoned her duties to listen to him speak. Vermeer treated this subject in *Christ in the House of Mary and Martha* (fig. 14), one of his earliest and most monumental paintings. Contemporary maids or kitchen servants also featured in many Dutch genre paintings at the time, significantly in works by Gerrit Dou (1613–1675) and his followers from the 1640s onward (fig. 15).

Vermeer may have had Dou's works in mind when he painted his *Milkmaid* (fig. 16).[42] She is more properly a kitchen maid, since milkmaids (while also the subject of paintings) were dairy workers who either worked on farms or made door-to-door deliveries of fresh milk in towns and cities. Vermeer's underlying intention in *The Milkmaid,* beyond making a virtuosic painting that renders every material texture and lighting effect with exquisite precision, is unclear. Her mental focus is striking, however, and has led some to see a certain sense of the heroic in his presentation of a member of the working class as the subject of a single-figure painting. Vermeer does not paint the occupation so much as the person herself, enhancing our apprehension of her as an autonomous individual.

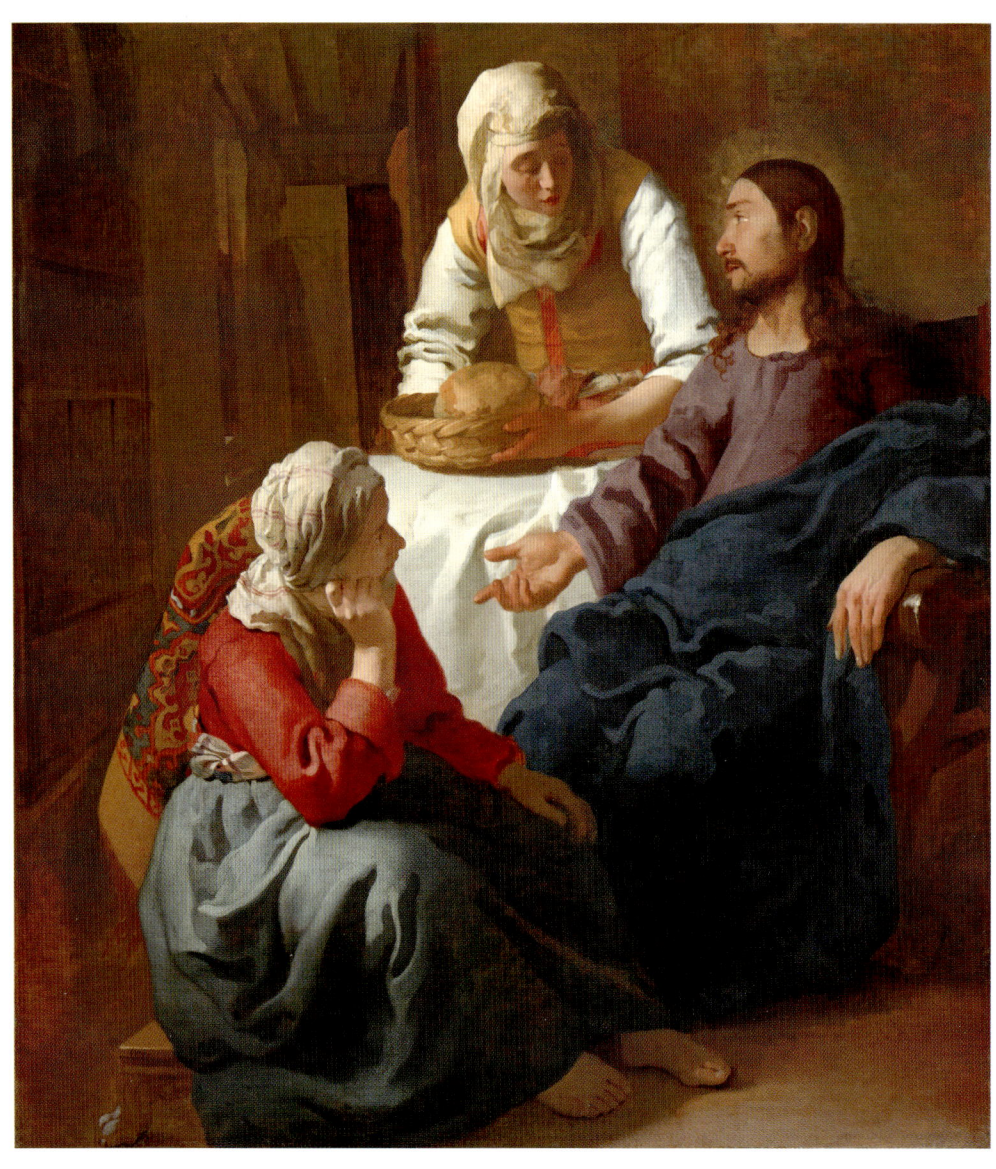

FIG. 14
Johannes Vermeer
Christ in the House of Mary and Martha, ca. 1654–55
Oil on canvas, 62⅜ × 55¹¹⁄₁₆ in. (158.5 × 141.5 cm)
National Galleries of Scotland, Edinburgh

Vermeer made one other painting that takes a maid as its singular subject, but it is set in a different key altogether—his *Maid Asleep* from around 1656–57 (fig. 17). In a 1696 auction catalogue, the subject is described as "a drunken, sleeping maid at a table."[43] Viewed out of context, we might question the assumptions that she is both drunk and a maid. Indeed, there was some question in earlier literature whether she might actually be the mistress of the house given her fashionable dress, jewelry, and makeup, complete with a *mouche*, or beauty spot, on her temple. Vermeer, however, worked within an already established tradition of portraying the supposed laziness of servants, one example of which is *The Idle Servant* by Nicolaes Maes (fig. 18), painted just a few years earlier.[44] The dress in Vermeer's painting was also not unusual for a maid at the time. One sees maids clothed similarly to the lady of the house in a number of other paintings, for example, in De Hooch's *Interior with Women by a Linen Cabinet* (fig. 19).[45] It was presumably up to the maid's employer to determine her level of dress, but it appears that ladies would often give maids their cast-off clothing, which, though perhaps just slightly out-of-date, might still be more expensive and fashionable than anything the maids could afford.

There has been some confusion as to who is who in De Hooch's painting.[46] The most likely convention is that the lady of the house (on the left) would wear a white apron, while the working servant's would be dyed a color that would hide stains, roles that conform with the maid being the bearer of the stack of linen. The same challenge we observe here in trying to distinguish mistress from maid in a painting proved to be a matter of concern for people in the seventeenth century. In 1682, the city of Amsterdam passed an ordinance that included sumptuary regulations for maids.[47] They were no longer to wear silk or other fancy clothing but were expected to dress simply, in accordance with their station, since codes of dress were vital for normalizing status distinctions.[48] Vermeer, like his contemporaries, offered paintings of maids dressed both ways: modestly in *The Milkmaid* and at or near the height of fashion in *A Maid Asleep*. The difference was not necessarily a judgmental one in the hands of painters, which is plain to see in De Hooch's *Interior with Women by a Linen Cabinet*, which clearly promotes the salutary nature of Dutch domestic life. Interesting in De Hooch's case is that records show the artist was once a servant in the employ of a linen merchant while maintaining his occupation as a painter.[49]

The maids in Vermeer's three love-letter paintings (cats. 1–3), perhaps using the same model, are dressed almost identically in relatively simple clothing. Each wears a rather plain brown bodice that contrasts nicely with her beautiful dark blue apron. This may have been a relatively common form of maid's dress in Holland in the 1660s. One finds it, for example, in a number of paintings by Metsu, such as his *Man Visiting a Woman Washing Her Hands* (fig. 20).[50] As in Metsu's works, Vermeer's use of dress in his love-letter paintings keeps the status distinction between the figures clear.

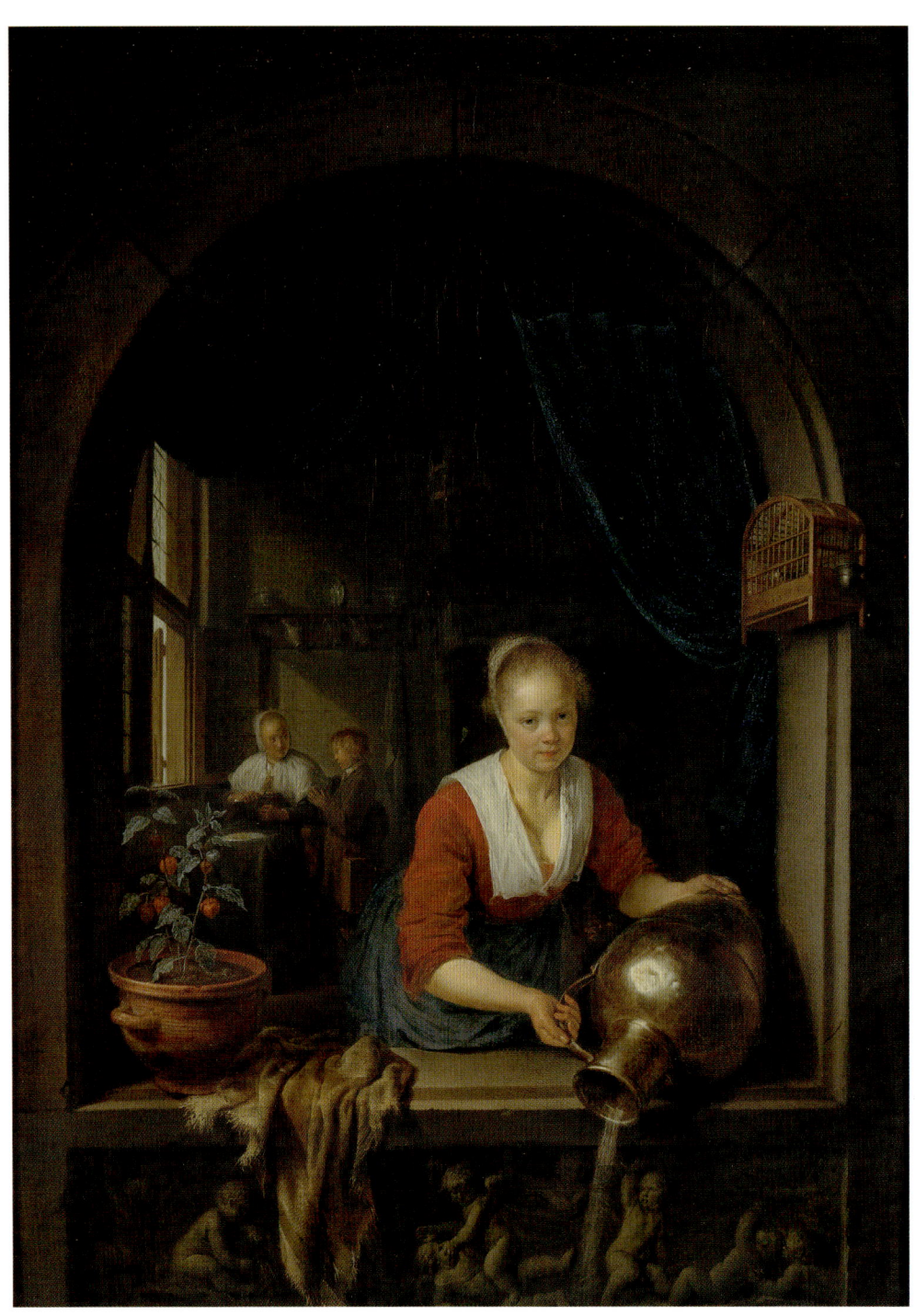

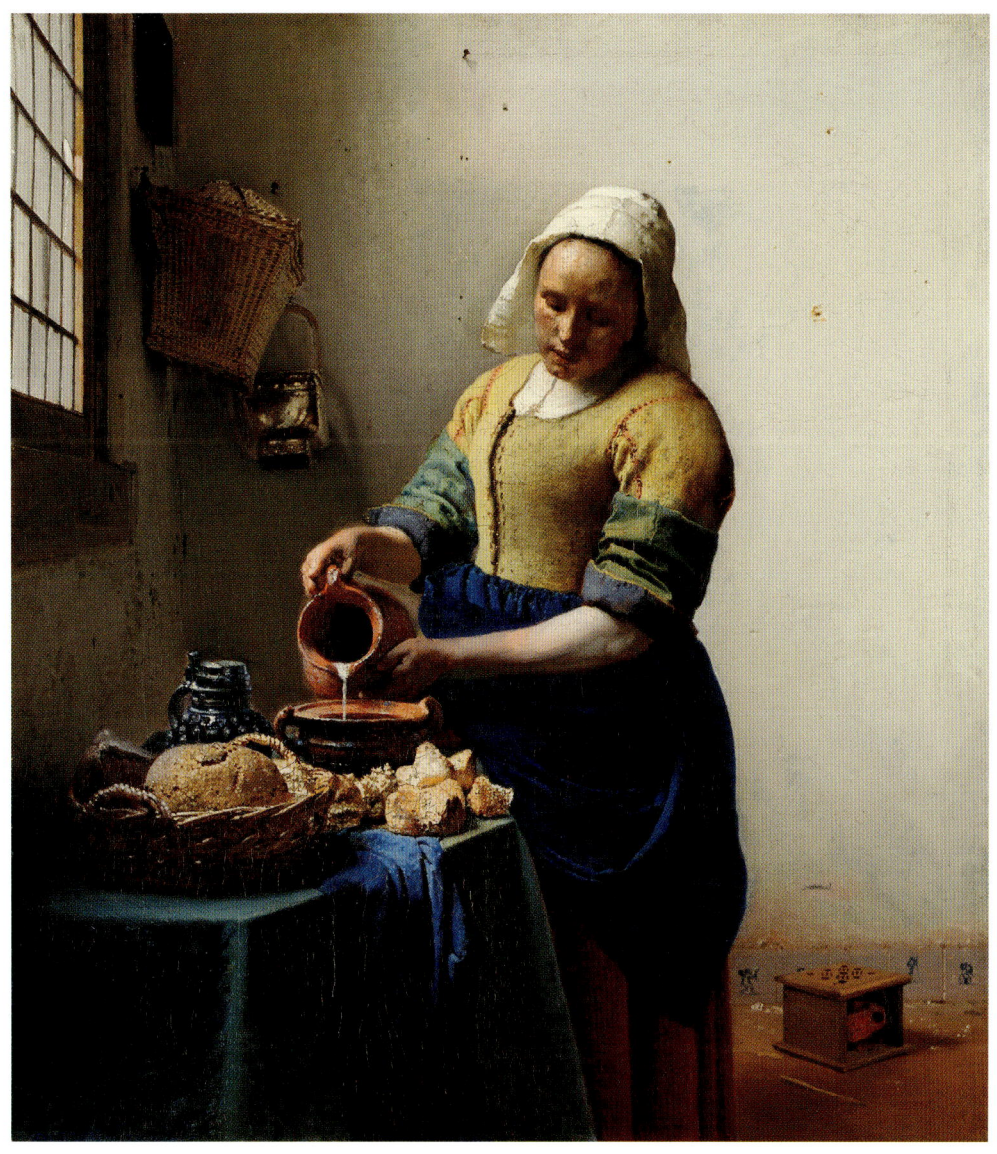

FIG. 15
Gerrit Dou
Maidservant at a Window, ca. 1660
Oil on canvas, 14¹⁵⁄₁₆ × 11 in. (38 × 28 cm)
Museum Boijmans Van Beuningen, Rotterdam

FIG. 16
Johannes Vermeer
The Milkmaid, ca. 1658–59
Oil on canvas, 17¹⁵⁄₁₆ × 16⅛ in. (45.5 × 41 cm)
Rijksmuseum, Amsterdam

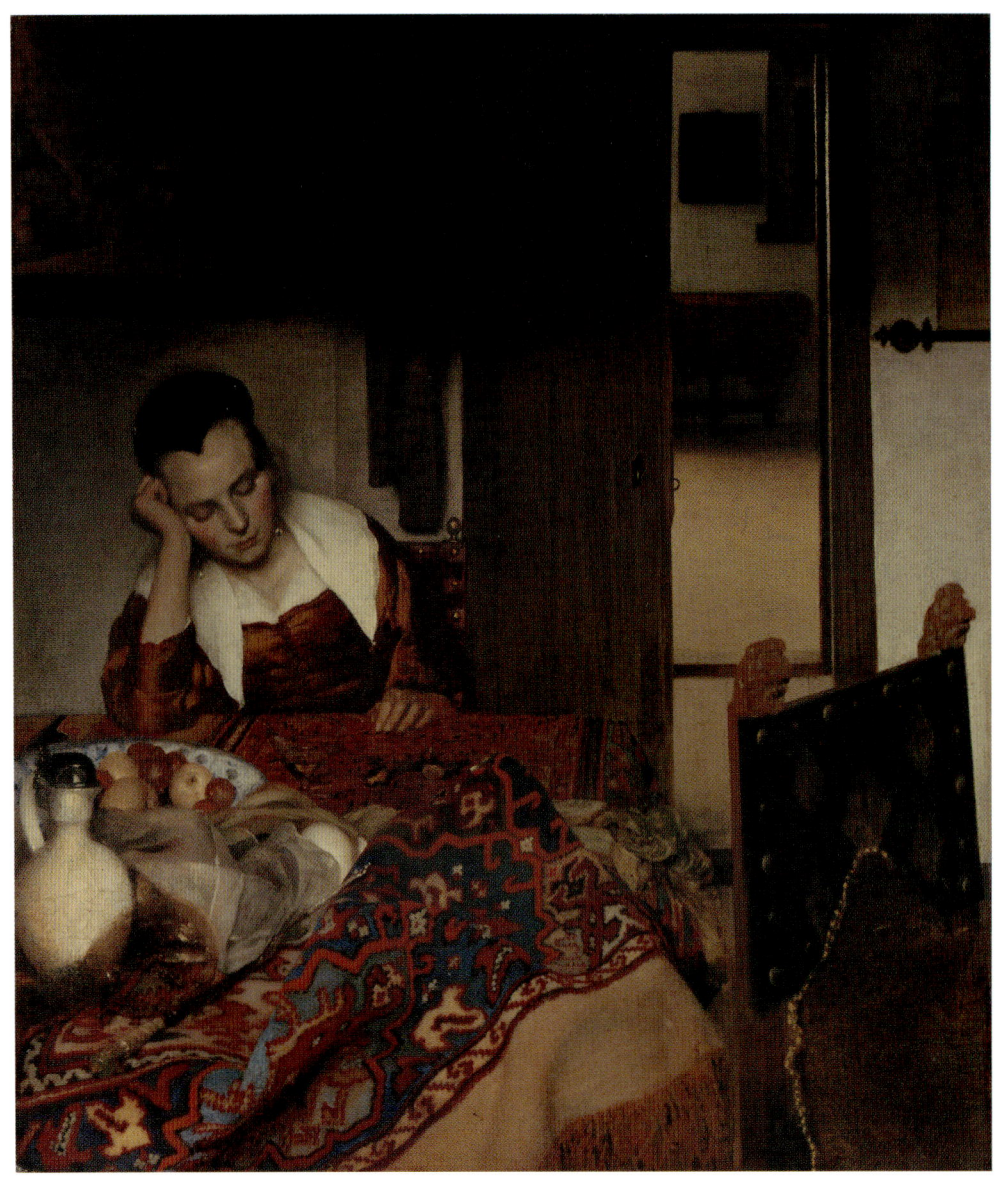

FIG. 17

Johannes Vermeer

A Maid Asleep, ca. 1656–57

Oil on canvas, 34½ × 30⅛ in. (87.6 × 76.5 cm)

The Metropolitan Museum of Art, New York

FIG. 18

Nicolaes Maes

The Idle Servant, 1655

Oil on panel, 27⁹⁄₁₆ × 21 in. (70 × 53.3 cm)

The National Gallery, London

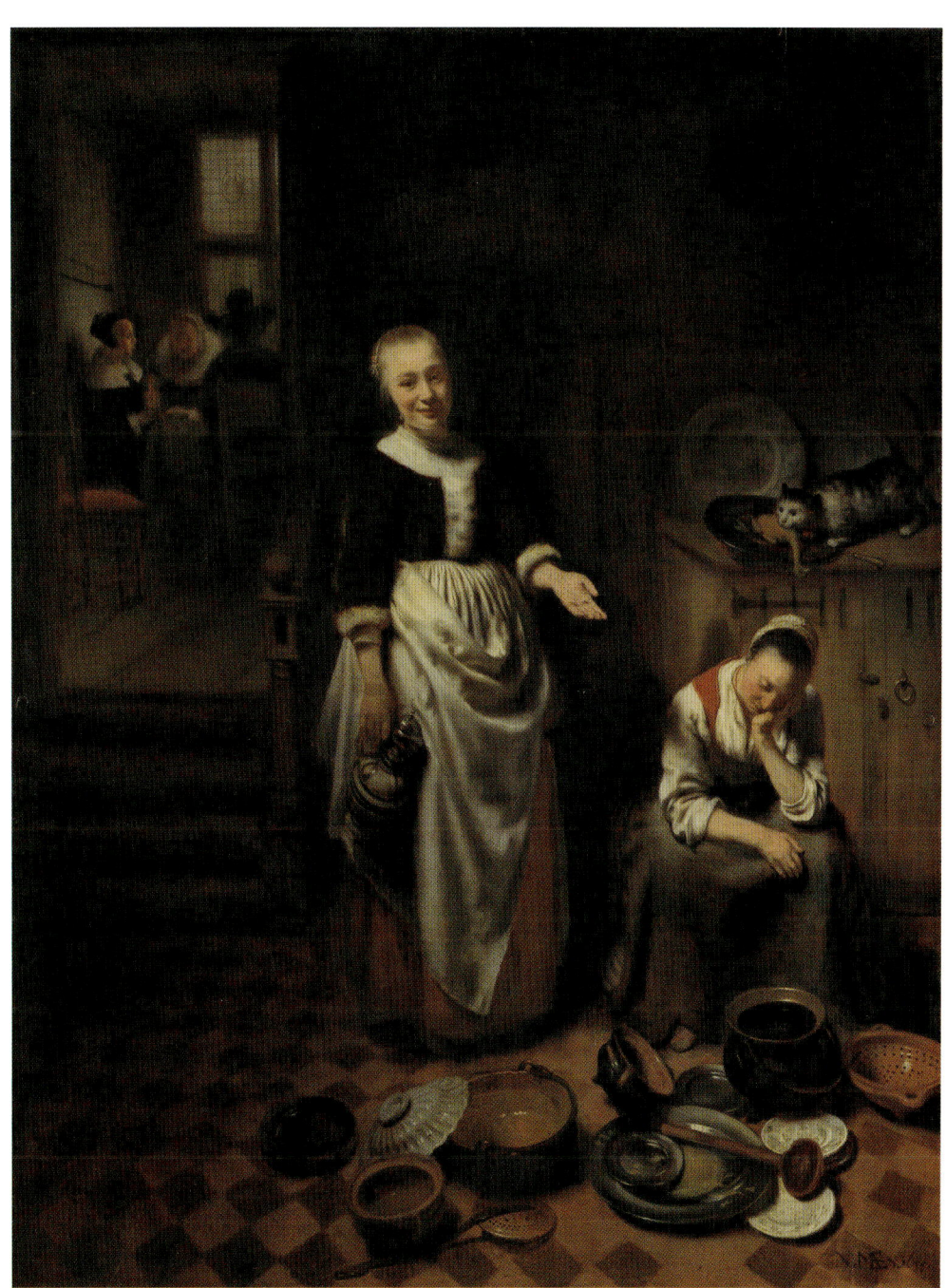

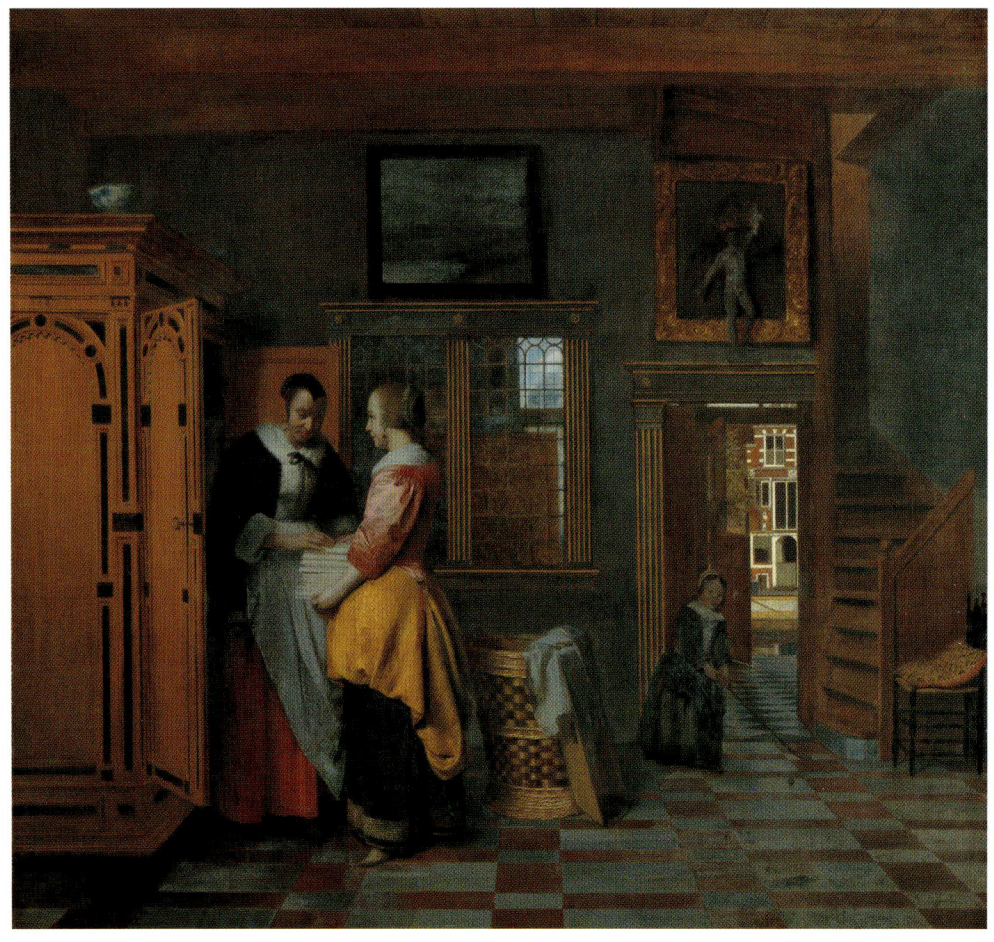

FIG. 19
Pieter de Hooch
Interior with Women by a
Linen Cabinet, 1663
Oil on canvas, 27⁹⁄₁₆ × 29¾ in. (70 × 75.5 cm)
Rijksmuseum, Amsterdam

FIG. 20
Gabriel Metsu
A Man Visiting a Woman Washing
Her Hands, ca. 1663–66
Oil on canvas, 32¹⁵⁄₁₆ × 26⁹⁄₁₆ in. (83.7 × 67.4 cm)
Waddesdon Manor, The Rothschild Collection

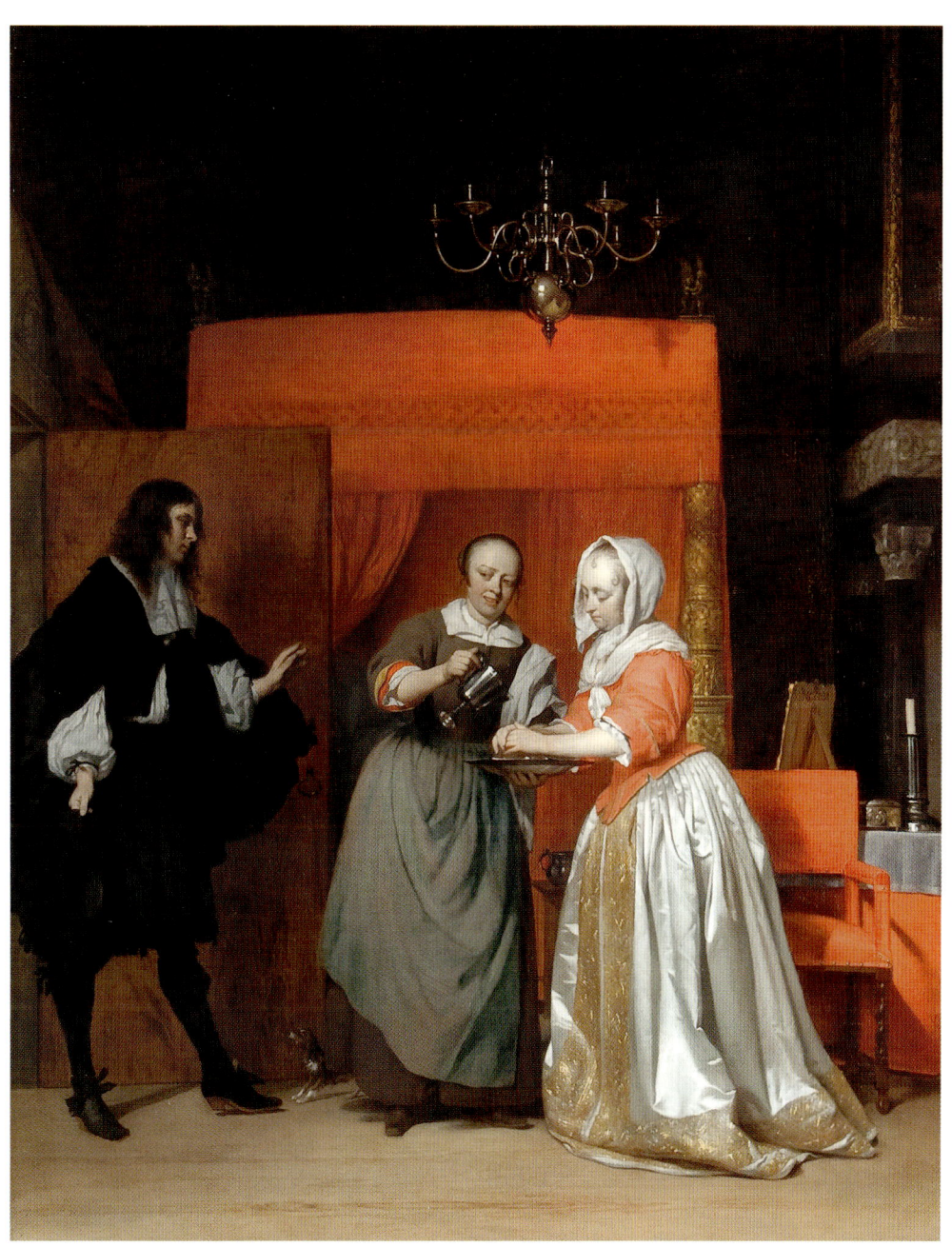

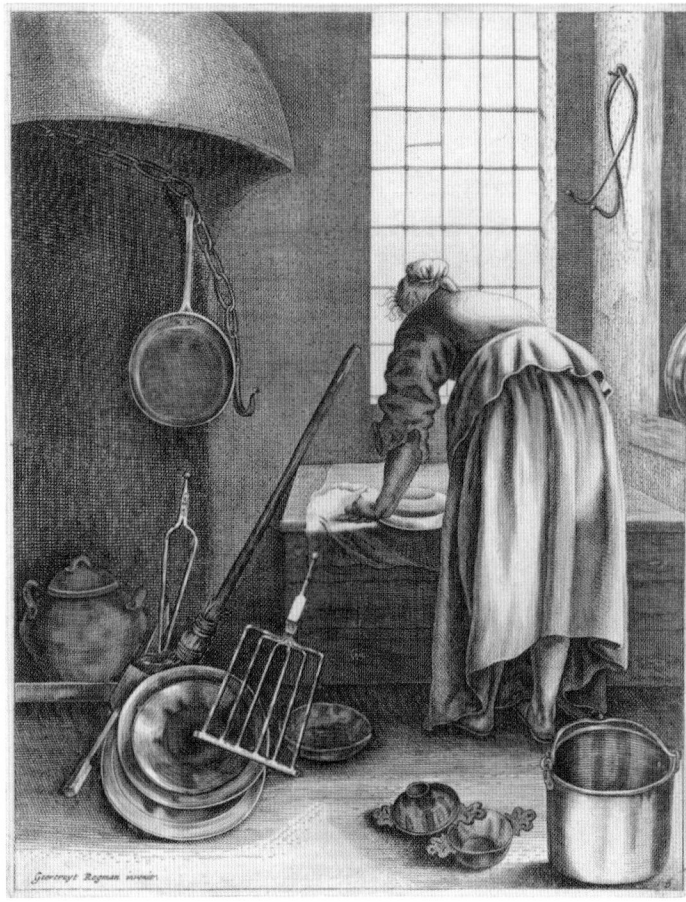

Seven Devils and Seven Angels

In Dutch genre paintings from the era, maids could be cast in a variety of roles. In one of the earliest studies of the subject in 1980, Simon Schama pointed to the "versions of womanhood" offered by various domestic scenes that operate along established polarities, sometimes stabilizing, sometimes disruptive, but always fabricated using images mediated by male perception.[51] All the more valuable, then, are the unparalleled images of contemporary domestic service made by a woman, Geertruydt Roghman (1625–1657), who created a rare series of five prints showing women at work.[52] The women are lost in their tasks, focused but unidealized. Sometimes Roghman depicts them from behind, which only serves to increase the sense of her subjects' anonymity within the household (fig. 21). Vermeer may well have encountered these prints, especially since he approaches their atmospheric quality in a work like *The Milkmaid*. In this iconic painting, a female domestic servant can stand as a central subject instead of a secondary one, without conforming to the norms of the existing visual tradition, in which some degree of

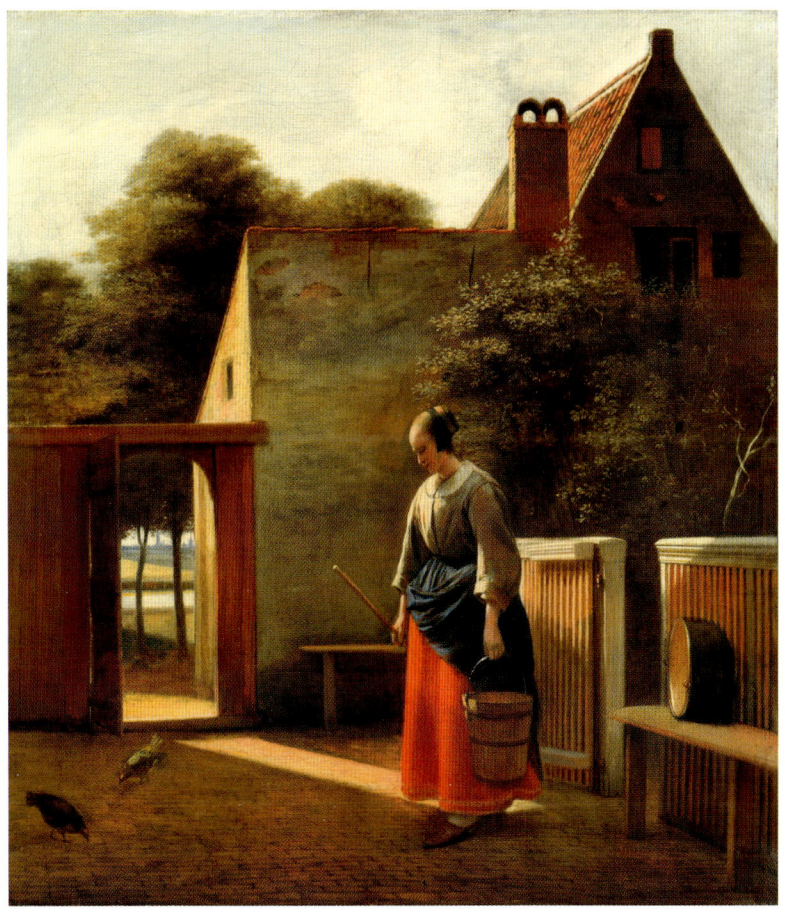

moral judgment or comic effect is implicit in renderings of maids. De Hooch also made a few autonomous images of maids that seem remarkably free from prescribed characterizations, such as his *Woman with a Bucket in a Courtyard* (fig. 22).[53]

The contemporary literature on maids, however, could be deeply critical. In 1682, the Utrecht schoolmaster and prolific writer Simon de Vries (ca. 1624–1708) published his *Seven Duyvelen, Regerende de Hedensdaeghsche Dienst-Maegden* (Seven Devils Ruling Present-Day Maidservants), in which he devoted surprisingly long chapters to each of the most common "sins" of maids, such as promiscuity, thievery, slander, and gluttony.[54] De Vries based his publication on a German book (*Sieben Böse Geister, welche heutiges Tages Knechte und Mägde regieren und verfuren*) that first appeared in Hamburg in the 1650s and which he thought would be fitting for a Dutch audience.[55] It must have been popular, as it quickly went into a second printing. Tellingly, however, the same publisher issued a different version of the book the same year by an anonymous author, who signed with the sobriquet Liefhebber van Dienstmaagden

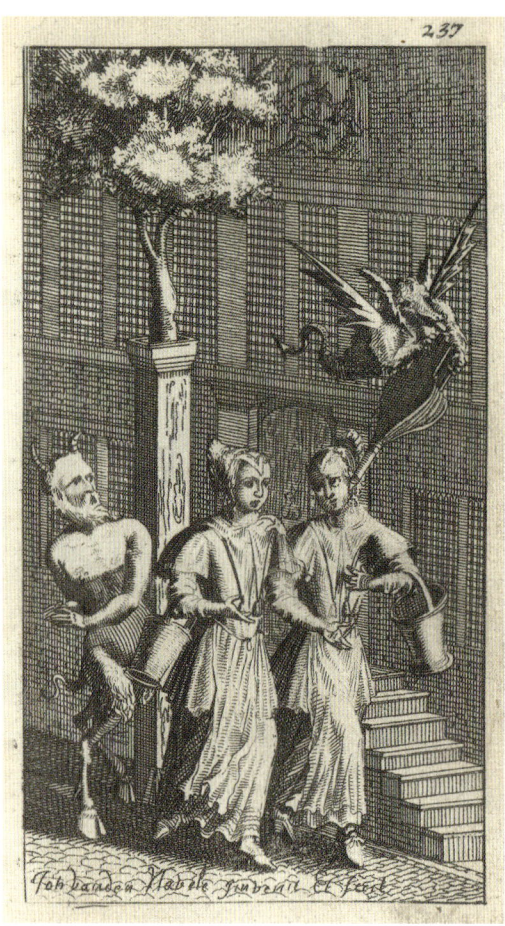

(literally, a "connoisseur of maids," which we can take to mean an authority on tales about them). It is similarly titled and organized, but its many anecdotes are cast in a manner suitable for a more salacious rather than moralizing type of reading.[56] Apparently, potential buyers could also choose to read titillating stories about maids purely as popular literature, without the sermonizing and biblical references that pepper De Vries's version.

De Vries and his anonymous counterpart do not discuss the passing of letters between a mistress and her lover as part of their highly negative critiques, but they do include a chapter titled "De Snap en Aghterklap Duyvel" (The Gossip and Slander Devil), in which the unreliability of maids in matters of privacy becomes paramount.[57] In the illustration for De Vries's chapter, two maids walk down the street with their market pails (*marktemmers*), no doubt gossiping about the goings-on in their employers' houses (fig. 23).[58] A demon uses a bellows to blow evil thoughts into the ear of one, while the devil standing next to the other has the temerity to express shock at the words he hears. The same year these books appeared, the city of Amsterdam issued its ordinance (perhaps inspired by these publications) regarding the acceptable behavior

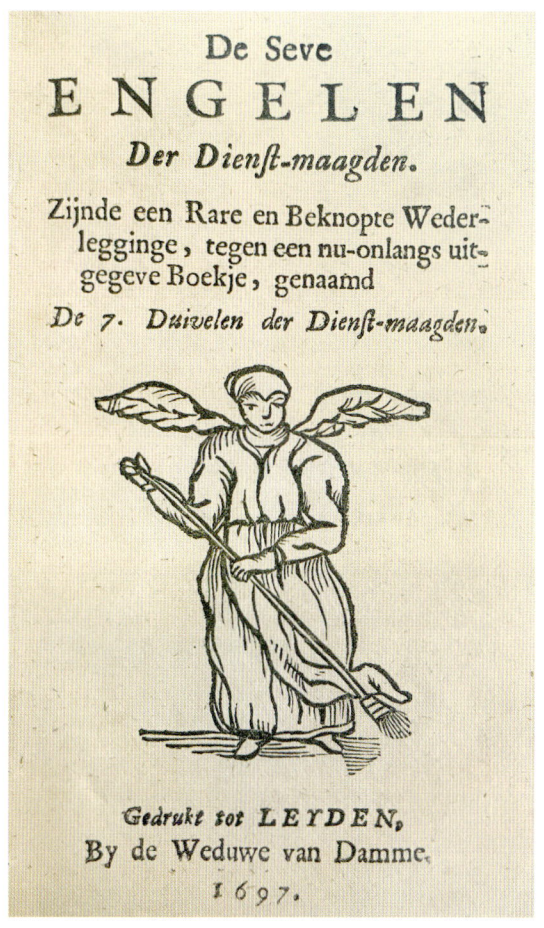

De Seve
ENGELEN
Der Dienft-maagden.

Zijnde een Rare en Beknopte Wederlegginge, tegen een nu-onlangs uitgegeve Boekje, genaamd

De 7. Duivelen der Dienft-maagden.

Gedrukt tot LEYDEN,
By de Weduwe van Damme.
1697.

of maids, including their level of dress, as mentioned above.[59] One of the stipulations was that maids were forbidden from discussing any private matters overheard in the household, such as arguments between the husband and wife. To do so was punishable by a three-month sentence in the Spinhuis.[60] Presumably, gossip about love affairs would likewise risk offense.

Seducing a member of the household was an even more serious infraction, punishable by a six-month sentence. Widowers were deemed particularly susceptible in this regard (Rembrandt comes to mind), though such an ordinance completely ignores the often complex realities of these relationships when they arise—or who initiates them in the first place.[61] Leaping to the rescue in this and other matters was the anonymous author of *De Seve Engelen Der Dienst-maagden* (The Seven Angels of Maidservants) (fig. 24).[62] As the title suggests, it was a direct response to the versions of the *Seven Duyvelen* and takes a mocking tone toward those publications. Known only in a single edition with a few surviving copies, it was not likely to have been read widely at the time but deserves more attention since it offers a missing counterbalance in the literary tradition (comparable to that in the visual tradition).[63] Its many observations about the realities of the life of a maidservant are especially poignant. Maids must deal with seducers, for example, and angry employers. If you consider them lazy, the author reasons with us, think about how many tasks they actually have to perform to keep the household running. If you consider them gossips, think about how difficult it can be to go days at a stretch without leaving the house and how natural it is to desire conversation when you do, especially to compare notes with other maids.[64] Furthermore, if you send them out at ten o'clock at night to deliver a message, they might have to fend off the young men looking for love (the Venus *jonkers*), sometimes physically pushing them off, as they wend their way back home.[65] Given the high degree of relatability of these stories, one cannot help wondering if the anonymous author of this remarkable tract was a woman.[66]

As extreme as this literature seems in either condemning or defending maids and their occupation, the experience that Vermeer and his family personally had with maids, according to archival sources, was as remarkably vivid as any literature on either side of the equation. The artist and his wife, Catharina Bolnes, lived with his affluent mother-in-law, Maria Thins, in a comfortably sized house in the small Catholic enclave in Delft called the Papenhoek (Papists' Corner). Sadly, Catharina's brother, Willem Bolnes, was a difficult individual (to put it mildly) who routinely harassed, verbally and even physically, both his sister and mother. In a deposition from 1666, Tanneke Everpoel, the maid of the house at the time, offered the following striking testimony:

> Today there appeared before Frans Boogert, notary in Delft, Willem de Coorde, Gerrit Cornelisz. stone carver, and Tanneke Everpoel, who testified at the request of Maria Thins that they were aware of the following facts. First, Tanneke Everpoel stated that in 1663 she had been residing at the house of the petitioner [Maria Thins] and of her son-in-law Johannes Vermeer. Tanneke and Gerrit Cornelisz. both declared that on various occasions Willem Bolnes had created a violent commotion in the house—to such an extent that many people gathered before the door—as he swore at his mother, calling her an old popish swine, a she-devil, and other such ugly swearwords that, for the sake of decency, must be passed over. She, Tanneke, also saw that Bolnes had pulled a knife and tried to wound his mother with it. She declared further that Maria Thins had suffered so much violence from her son that she dared not go out of her room and was forced to have her food and drink brought there. Also that Bolnes committed similar violence from time to time against the daughter of Maria Thins, the wife of Johannes Vermeer, threatening to beat her on diverse occasions with a stick, notwithstanding the fact that she was pregnant to the last degree. The witness added that this would have happened had she not prevented it.[67]

In other words, Everpoel had to intervene physically to prevent Willem from beating the highly pregnant Catharina. Everpoel's bodily protection was certainly heroic, but depositions of this kind were not uncommon. Maids were routinely called upon to testify in cases of domestic violence.

Shortly after this deposition, Thins received permission from the Delft magistrate to have her son confined, committing him to the house of a certain Hermanus Taerling, who specialized in taking in "delinquent and mentally ill persons."[68] But the story does not end there. Taerling had a maidservant, Mary Gerrits, who became betrothed to Willem during his confinement. Once banns publicly announcing their engagement were posted, Thins set in motion a campaign to block her son's marriage to this woman she later called "a notorious person and a thief."[69] Among the depositions is one describing an attempt by Gerrits to force the marriage to take place by faking her pregnancy, with one witness testifying that "she had for some time bound a cushion to her belly to induce these relatives to believe she was pregnant."[70] Evidence of her thievery also emerged. The stakes were obviously high for Thins, along with Vermeer and his family, since she would have had to split her estate more substantially with Willem had he borne children. Thins's efforts, in the end, succeeded. Gerrits went so far as to sue Thins, still hoping for the hand of Willem; but by that point, he was no longer deceived, stating that "he would rather have a millstone around his neck and [be] thrown into the sea than to marry her" and that "she would not marry him except for his money."[71] In any case, Gerrits lost the lawsuit and would not be heard from again. Exit devilish maid.

As for Everpoel, she appears to have entered into Thins's service a few years earlier, around 1661–62. In her testament drawn up on May 14, 1662, Thins deeded 20 guilders to her servant (not mentioned by name), provided that "the latter will have lived with her [for at least] three years before her death and have deserved the bequest, to the discretion of Catharina."[72] Her caution is perhaps understandable; but in any case, it suggests that the servant was relatively new to the household. At some point the following year, the incident took place in which she defended Catharina from a beating by Willem, so we can assume that it was Everpoel whom Thins referred to in her testament—and that she later earned her bequest. Many years later, shortly after Vermeer died in 1675, Everpoel is listed among his widow's creditors in the sad financial aftermath of the artist's death.[73] She appears to have faithfully served Vermeer's family for well over ten years.

There has been an occasional, though persistent, trend in art-historical literature to posit Tanneke Everpoel as the model Vermeer used for *The Milkmaid*. When John Michael Montias promoted this idea in his groundbreaking, archivally based study of Vermeer's life in 1989, some scholars still thought the painting should be dated somewhat later, in the early 1660s.[74] Based on stylistic criteria, however, this painting is now thought to have been made around 1658–59. Most likely, Everpoel was not a member of the household until the early 1660s. If Vermeer was inclined to use her as a model, then she more likely features as the maid in his love-letter paintings, all thought to have been painted between 1664 and 1672. The figure with similar features certainly seems recognizable from one painting to the next. While there is no certain evidence of this, nor of any figure from Vermeer's family being used in one of his paintings, we know that artists at the time did not hesitate to engage household members as dramatis personae for their staged inventions. If Vermeer did make use of Everpoel as a model, one hopes she appreciated the experience, much as the artist must have appreciated her apparent devotion to the family.

CHAPTER 3

Modern Love

LOVE-LETTER-THEMED PAINTINGS with a young woman and a maid together began to appear in the late 1650s. Once again, as with paintings of single-figure women writing letters, Ter Borch appears to have led the way. The earliest of these works might be his *Woman Sealing a Letter with a Maidservant* from around 1658–59 (fig. 26).[75] The date is based on the fact that its companion piece, *Officer Writing a Letter with a Trumpeter* (fig. 25), uses Ter Borch's pupil, Caspar Netscher (1639–1684), as a model for the officer, before he set out on his own around 1659.[76] These two progenitors of the letter-and-servant motif, in this case male and female, were not recognized as being pendants until relatively recently.[77]

In *Officer Writing a Letter with a Trumpeter*, the ace-of-hearts card lying on the ground provides a visual clue for the viewer as to the nature of the officer's missive. Creating a pair of paintings around the exchange of letters between a man and a woman cleverly thematizes the notion of written courtship by letter writers in separate locations. Ter Borch clearly enjoyed using similar settings and props within the paintings, rearranging the chimney and mantel, for example, and placing similarly green-curtained beds in the background. They even share a table with the same repair (a lighter pine plank) between its feet, a detail that would have amused astute viewers if the paintings once hung together. The maid in *Woman Sealing a Letter* carries a *marktemmer* (market pail) on her arm, clearly signaling her status as a servant and also her connection to the outside world, where the letter must go.

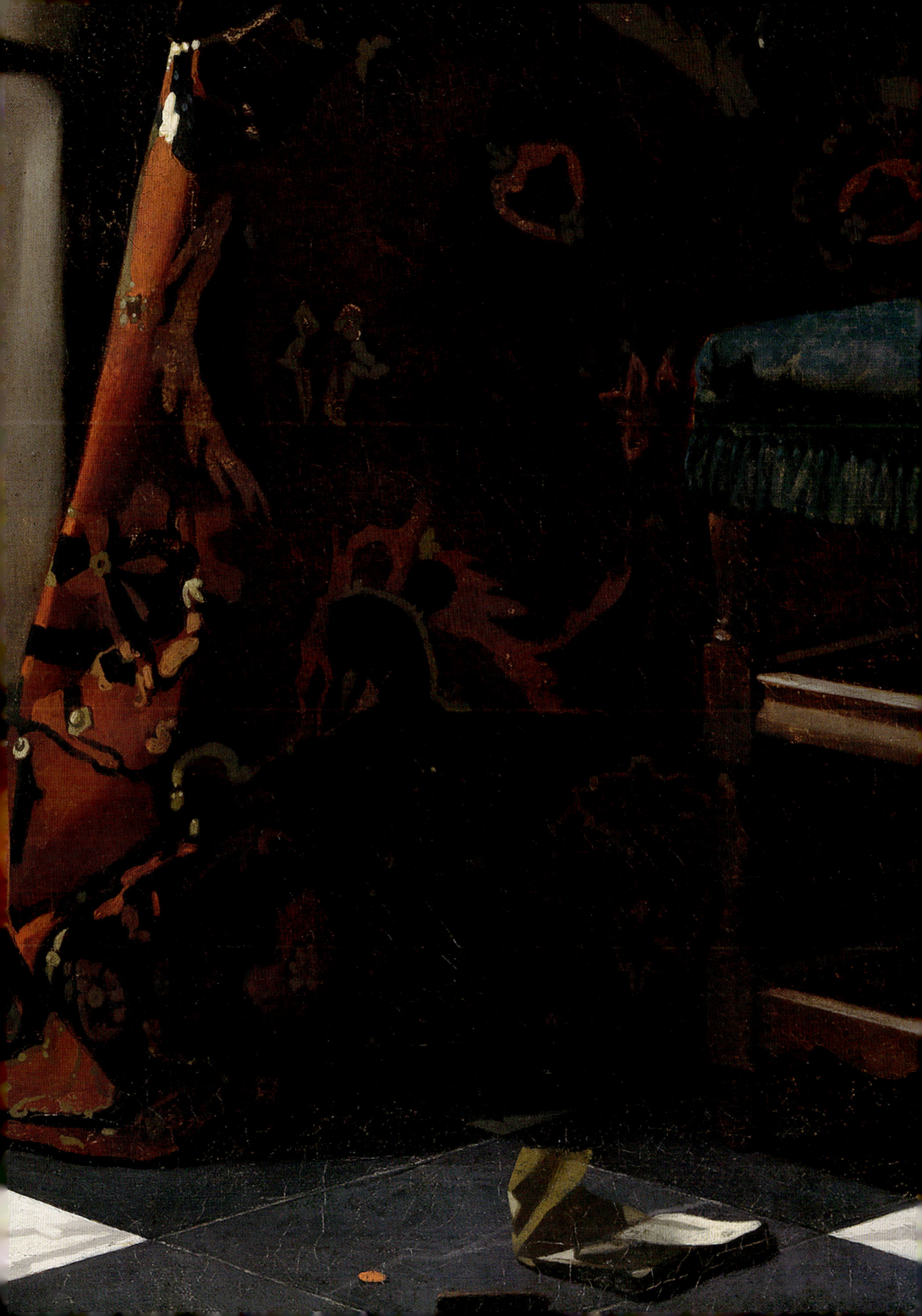

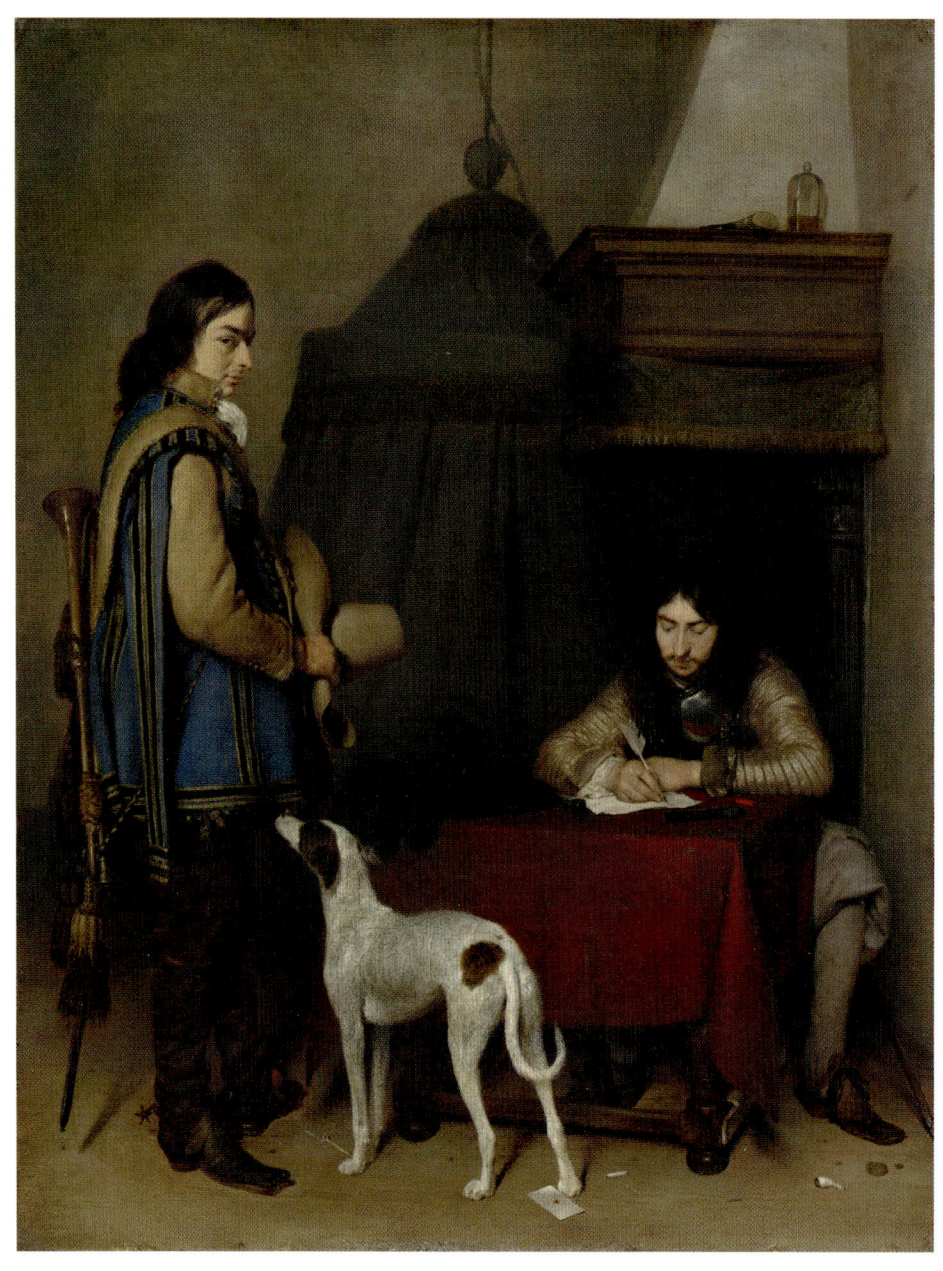

FIG. 25

Gerard ter Borch

Officer Writing a Letter with a Trumpeter, ca. 1658–59

Oil on canvas, 22⅜ × 17¼ in. (56.8 × 43.8 cm)

Philadelphia Museum of Art

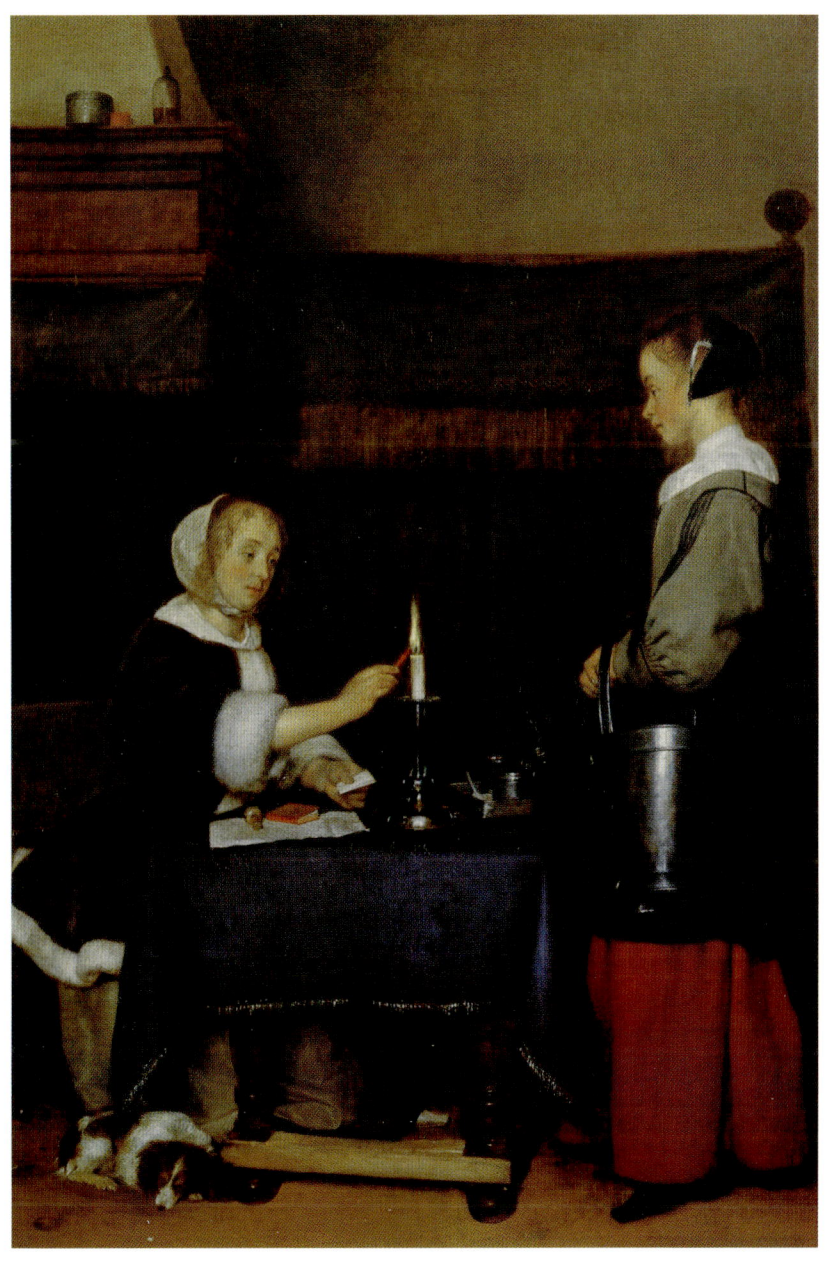

FIG. 26
Gerard ter Borch
Woman Sealing a Letter with a Maidservant (detail), ca. 1658–59
Oil on canvas, 22¼ × 17¼ in. (56.5 × 43.8 cm)
Private collection, New York

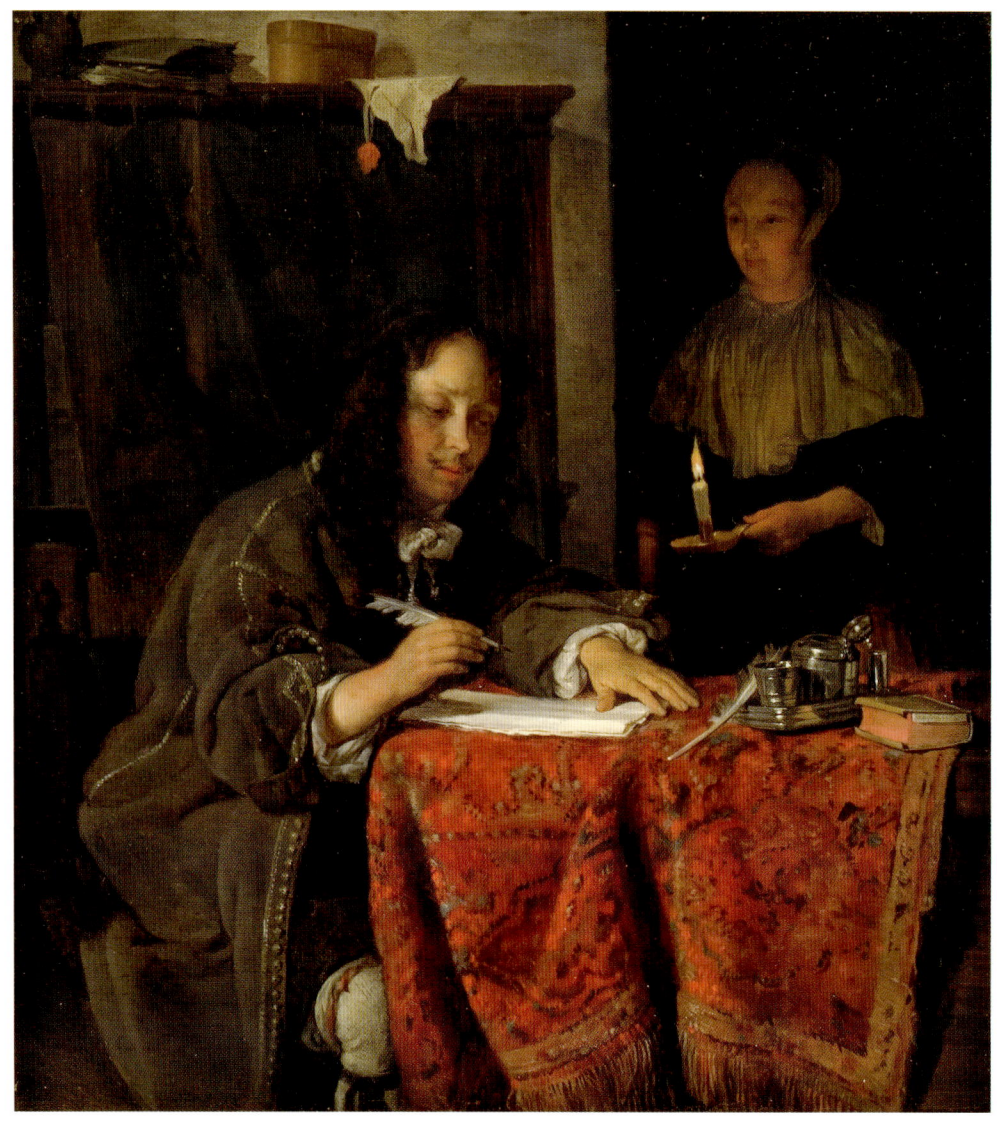

FIG. 27
Gabriel Metsu
Man Writing a Letter, ca. 1658–60
Oil on panel, 11 × 10¼ in. (28 × 26 cm)
Musée Fabre, Montpellier

FIG. 28
Gabriel Metsu
Girl Receiving a Letter, ca. 1658–60
Oil on panel, 10⅛ × 9⅝ in. (25.7 × 24.4 cm)
Timken Museum of Art, San Diego

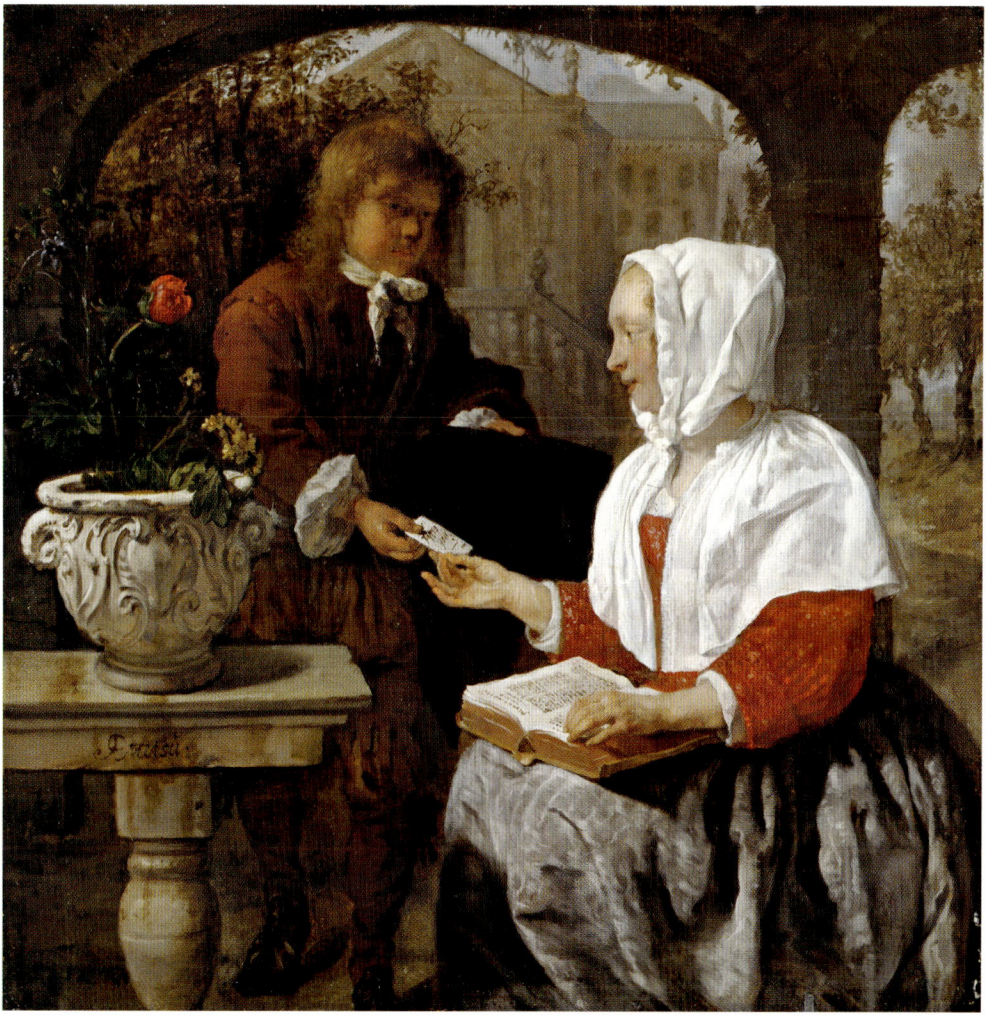

Metsu picked up on the idea of paired letter writers for two smaller works he made soon thereafter (figs. 27, 28).[78] He reversed the genders of the servants, with a young man bringing a woman a letter upon which the word *juffr.* (for *juffrouw*, or lady) can be seen. For the main figures, Metsu used the likenesses of himself and his wife, Isabella de Wolff, who was the daughter of the painter Maria de Grebber (1602–1680). Metsu often used De Wolff as a model, but one wonders if this particular pair of paintings was personal, perhaps a testament to their love. Stylistic analysis suggests that he painted these shortly after their marriage in 1658, which, of course, would not exclude a love theme even if their period of courtship was over.

A few years later, Metsu executed two of his great masterpieces, the pendant paintings *Man Writing a Letter* (fig. 29) and *Woman Reading a Letter* (fig. 30).[79] Both figures appear lost in thought. True to the concept of paired images, Metsu conveyed their intimate connection

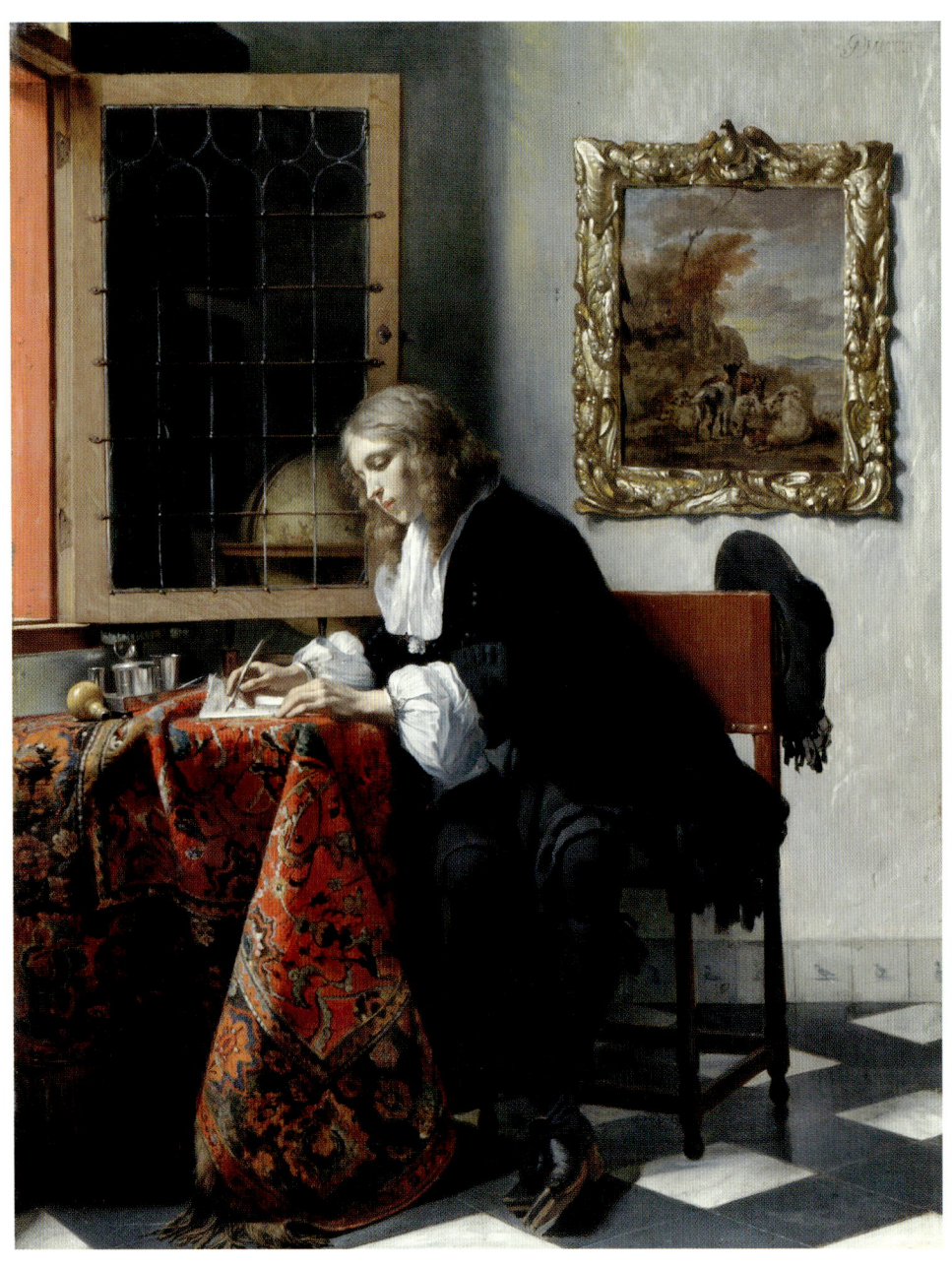

FIG. 29
Gabriel Metsu
Man Writing a Letter, ca. 1664–66
Oil on panel, 20¹¹⁄₁₆ × 15¹³⁄₁₆ in. (52.5 × 40.2 cm)
National Gallery of Ireland, Dublin

56

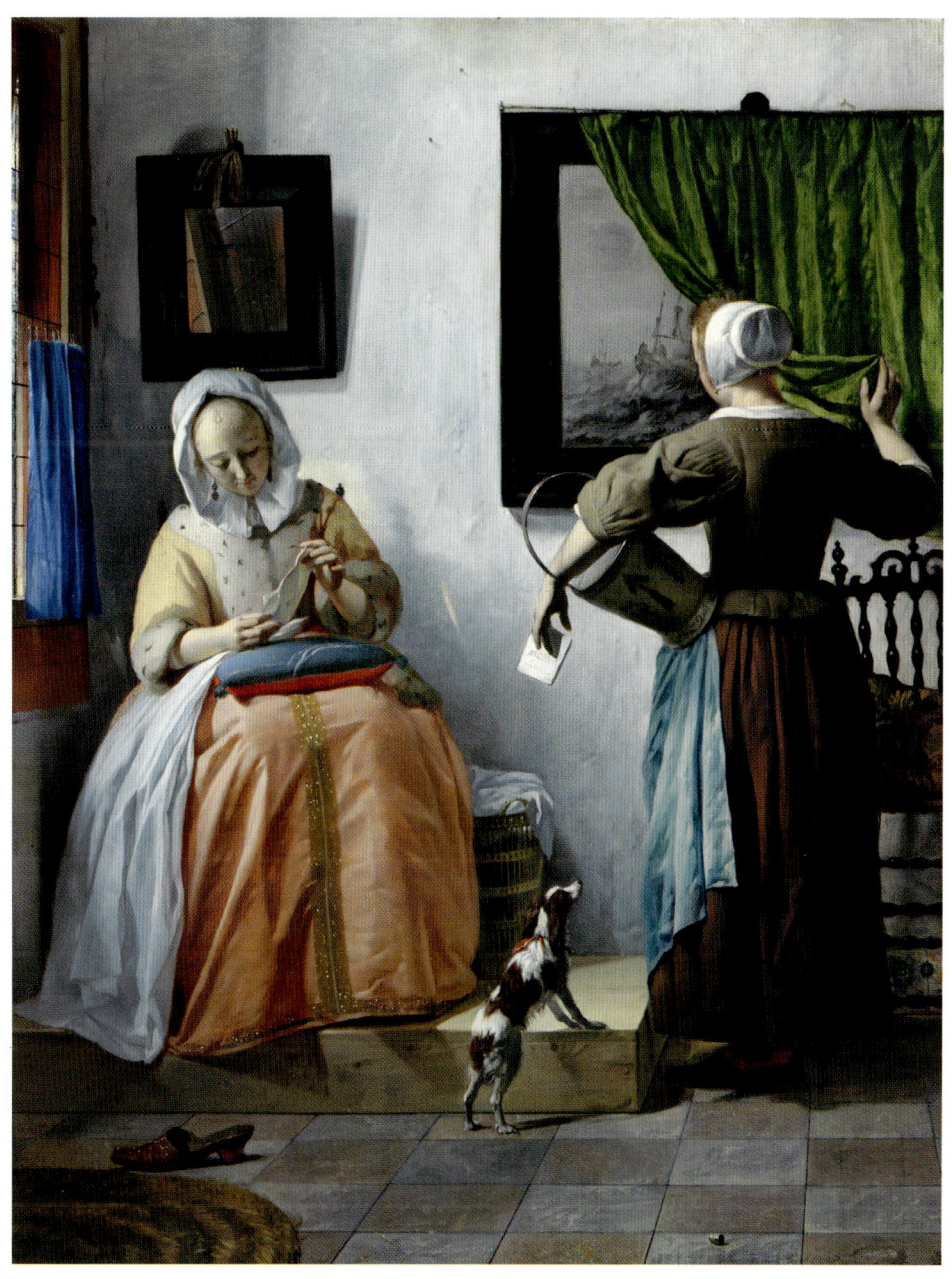

FIG. 30
Gabriel Metsu
Woman Reading a Letter, ca. 1664–66
Oil on panel, 20¹¹⁄₁₆ × 15¹³⁄₁₆ in. (52.5 × 40.2 cm)
National Gallery of Ireland, Dublin

through written exchange with works of art that he presumably intended to be physically proximate when hung together. In this case, the paintings managed, quite remarkably, to stay together as a pair for their entire existence, always having been in the same collection and now sharing their lives in the same museum. While there is no evidence that they depict an actual couple, the overall tenor is one of genuine affection, or at least they appear less staged than one finds in the paintings by Ter Borch. One of the most remarked-upon aspects of *Woman Reading a Letter* is that her maid lifts the curtain to a seascape painting while she waits. The stormy nature of the sea has naturally led some to make a connection to the perils of love, suggested by the tradition of showing seascapes behind letter writers as a reflection of mood. Negative feelings nevertheless seem incongruous with the generally positive atmosphere in this pair. Worth considering is a more direct reading of the maid's act, in which Metsu intended the uncovering of the painting to mirror the woman's act of opening the letter. Such a witticism plays on the simultaneous revelation of contents unknown and the anticipatory act of seeing for the first time.[80]

By contrast to these paired paintings, Vermeer's works focus on women. Love-letter-themed paintings featuring servants may have begun in the pendant format, revolving around the notion of the missing presence of a beloved, but there is no evidence that Vermeer ever planned or executed a male equivalent. His maids, furthermore, have dispensed with the market pail, perhaps as an overly obvious device (though one does appear hanging on the wall in the background of *The Milkmaid*). Vermeer's letter-and-maid paintings perform in their own distinct way, with great subtlety in acting out notions of uncertainty, expectation, and measured emotions.

His focus on women as writers of love letters is all the more significant given that contemporary moralistic literature for *vrysters* (young single women) suggests that they should keep their written efforts in courtship as circumspect as possible.[81] The most popular and widely read Dutch moralist of the seventeenth century, Jacob Cats (1577–1660), discouraged *vrysters* from writing letters to their objects of affection in his famous verse work *Houwelyck* (1625), a long prescriptive tract on the proper behavior for women throughout the various stages of their lives.[82] In a dialogue between the *vryster* Rosette and the newly married Sibille (her more experienced guide), Rosette asks:

> Imagine if I find a young man appealing,
> Shall I not sweetly, in a letter,
> Bemoan to him about my desire?
> Paper does not modestly blush,
> And pen and ink express in ways
> That mouth and tongue do not dare.[83]

Definitely not, warns Sibille. Anything that you commit to paper might ruin your good name since letters can have a life of their own once they leave your hands, and "There is no denial possible / when one sees your round letters standing there."

The dozens of editions of letter-writing manuals that circulated in Europe in the seventeenth century served as ancillary codes of conduct for any number of situations by providing sample letters that readers could use or modify according to the occasion, whether offering condolences, lodging a complaint, or celebrating an event.[84] A number of these manuals, including those in Dutch editions, contained sample love letters as well.[85] According to these manuals, which were stiff and florid in their prose, the man should always take the initiative. One of the most popular manuals, by Jean Puget de la Serre, suggests an opening salvo along the lines of "I must of necessity, for my own quiet, declare the desire which I have to love and serve you, if you judge me worthy of so great an honor."[86] Strikingly, but unsurprisingly, a woman's response must always exhibit restraint; she was usually expected to offer a polite refusal.[87] If she wanted to leave the door open for further pursuit, it must be done carefully. A suggested answer to the previous letter might be: "I am much obliged to you for the good will you witness on my behalf, but I have no other liberty left me, except to give you thanks, as I do very humbly."[88] Many of the proffered responses in the letter-writing manuals are, in fact, polite refusals. A good number also refer the suitor to the young woman's parents, whose approval, she makes clear, will determine the fate of their relationship.

One gets the sense that, even under ideal circumstances, letter writing between courting lovers who truly desired each other could be quite a literary challenge, particularly for women. The popular and highly regarded French novelist Madeleine de Scudéry (1607–1701), while approving of the gender distinction in love-letter writing in which women must remain more virtuous and modest in tone, noted that it paradoxically makes them better writers because they have to express desire without specifically stating it.[89] One imagines that the tone, as well as the content, could open up considerably once the couple were betrothed or married.[90]

Despite the constraints imposed by seventeenth-century mores on the outward expression of amorous female love, there was rich and effusive classical literature on the theme that enjoyed great popularity in Europe at the time, especially in the Netherlands.[91] It came in the form of Ovid's *Heroides* (also called the *Epistulae Heroidum*, or *Epistles of the Heroines*), a collection of imaginary letters from mythological figures to their lovers, such as Penelope to Ulysses, Dido to Aeneas, Ariadne to Theseus, and Helen to Paris, among others. The book was widely appreciated in the Middle Ages, though it remained accessible only to those who could read Latin until the sixteenth century, when the first vernacular translations began to appear (fig. 31).[92] The first complete Dutch translation in 1553 went by the title *Der Griecxser Princerssen* (The Greek Princesses).[93] It was quickly anthologized and turned into popular variants, such as the *Princesse Liet-Boec* (The Princess Songbook), a songbook published in Amsterdam in 1605.[94] The point of Ovid's text was to dramatize the complexities around the fortunes of love, whether desire or abandonment, longing or despair. Every letter reflects some sort of critical juncture in the relationship, moments of uncertainty that play ironically with the first-person epistolary form since we as readers presumably know the outcomes of these famous myths. But Ovid also took seriously the full expression of the range of emotions around love (albeit as a man, Ovid, embodying women), such as the grief of Ariadne after her abandonment by Theseus:

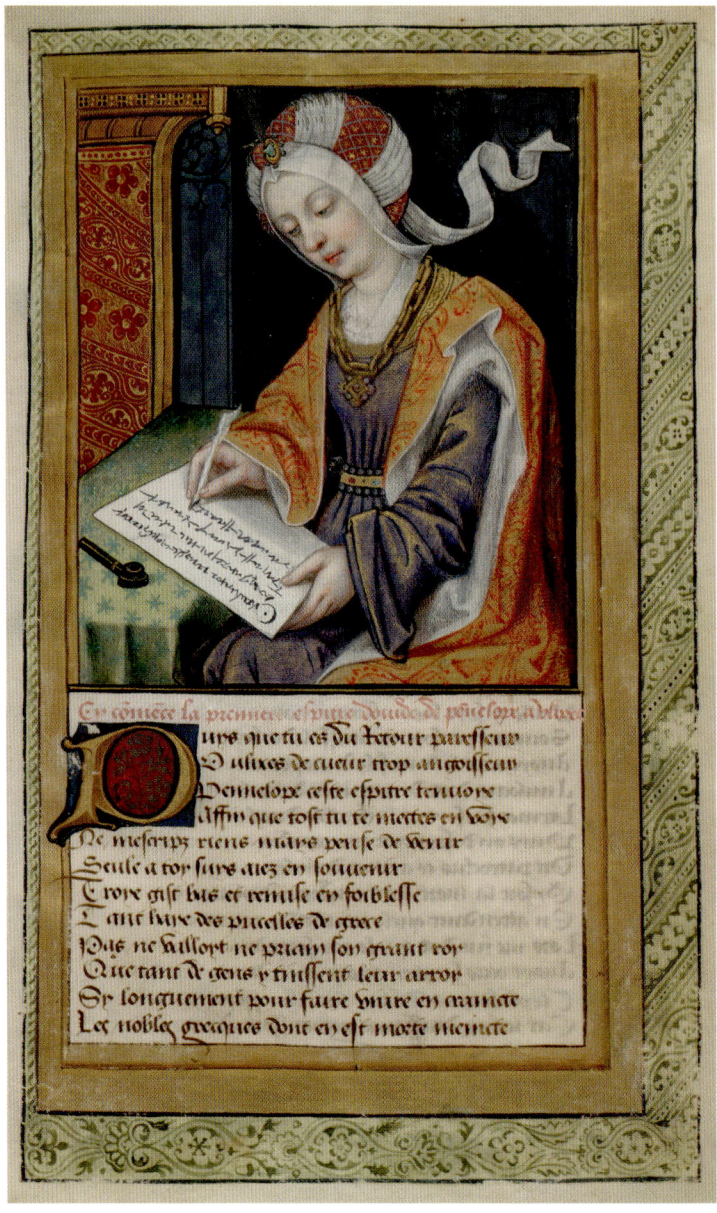

FIG. 31
Robinet Testard
Portrait of Penelope, from *Les XXI epistres des dames
illustes traduicttes d'Ovide*, ca. 1500
Illumination on parchment, 9⁹⁄₁₆ × 6⁹⁄₁₆ in. (243 × 167 mm)
The Huntington Library, Art Museum, and
Botanical Gardens, San Marino

If I had not saved you from danger, it would still be wrong for you to injure me.
These hands are weary of beating my sad breast, but I stretch them out to you across
the vast sea; what is left of my hair, in grief, I display and beg that you notice.[95]

There is nothing lighthearted about the situations that Ovid's women find themselves in, but the songbook variants transform them into something rather different, turning his meditations on the fortunes of love into merry and playful tunes for young, courting lovers (the main target audience of songbooks). With Ovid's *Heroides* in hand, however, we can also read the letter-writing paintings by Vermeer against the grain, not as relatively benign scenes of everyday life, charming in their simplicity, but as works that thematize the complexities of emotion that become internalized through the process of reading or writing letters. This is precisely the pretext of the *Heroides*, a literary work. Likewise, Vermeer's paintings do not necessarily intend to mirror reality so much as to dramatize it.

Another famous work by Ovid, arguably even more central to the production of paintings by Vermeer and other artists who treated the theme of love letters, is the *Ars Amatoria* (*The Art of Love*), a manual for courtship in all its forms.[96] Its first two chapters are devoted to men pursuing women, but the third chapter is addressed to women pursuing men. It has a complicated history in vernacular translation, in part due to its perceived function as a useful manual of seduction, with much content that many would no doubt consider immoral, dangerous, or too explicit in its unredacted form. Many educated young men, however, had access to the original Latin, making knowledge about the art of seduction itself greatly unbalanced between the genders, at least when it came to famed classical texts.

According to the *Ars Amatoria*, love letters were an essential component to seduction, the way to begin an affair and to sustain it. In Roman antiquity, of course, this meant writing on wax tablets. One must smooth the wax properly, Ovid advises men, else your lover might see the traces of letters you wrote to other women.[97] Maidservants (slaves at the time) also play a role in the *Ars Amatoria* as important go-betweens for both men and women. He advises women not to use too pretty a maid because he (Ovid) has on more than one occasion used her as a proxy lover.[98]

Vernacular translations tended to tone down Ovid's more roguish advice and to edit out the sexually explicit passages. At the end of Book Three, for example, Ovid gives specific advice to women about various sexual positions and how to determine what might suit them best.[99] The passage was left out of most (if not all) seventeenth-century Dutch translations, though it did appear in unexpurgated form in a highly popular English translation printed in Amsterdam early in the century.[100] Particular to certain Dutch translations, however, was an appendix with sample love letters, much like those that featured in the letter-writing manuals, with similar emotional restraint expected from the female side. The sample letters already appear in what is perhaps the earliest translation of the *Ars Amatoria* into Dutch, *De Conste der Minnen* from 1564, in which the translator states that the printer added the sample letters for the edification of the reader.[101] An Amsterdam edition from 1660 based on this translation even advertised on the title page "newly improved and edited, with even more new letters."[102]

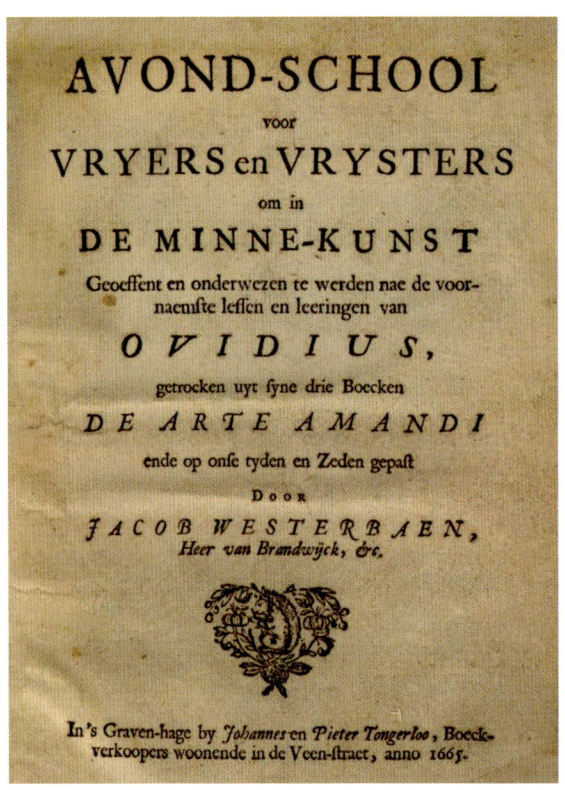

The most popular version of Ovid's *Ars Amatoria* in Vermeer's day was *Den Avond-School voor Vryers en Vrysters om in de Minne-Kunst . . .* (The Evening School for Single Men and Women in the Art of Love), published in 1665 by Jacob Westerbaen (1599–1670) (fig. 32), a popular poet and writer based in The Hague.[103] His was a heavily modified verse adaptation rather than a direct translation, which was not unusual when handling the *Ars Amatoria*. Fifty years earlier, Johan van Heemskerk (1597–1656) had already published a greatly condensed form of the *Ars Amatoria* as the *Minne-Kunst* (The Art of Love), which, while greatly toned down, still aimed to remain didactic in function, playfully advising young men and women in rhymed verses on the ins and outs of courtship.[104] Van Heemskerk provided brief advice on letter writing, advising his readers to take care that their letters not be seen by others and to write in a manner that will keep their hand unrecognizable. When Westerbaen took up the challenge in Vermeer's lifetime, he made even more explicit his desire to modernize Ovid's text, stating in the foreword:

> He [Ovid] was the old boss who described in a time long past,
> How in ancient Rome one might court a woman the best.
> Well, I thought, why not do so with The Hague in mind?

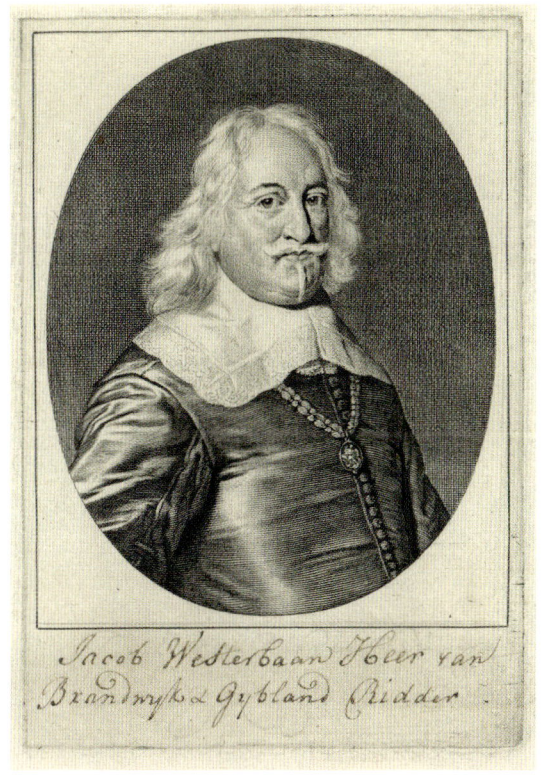

And thus I have Roman clothing torn and sliced,
For our own peoples, lengthened, shortened, adjusted, and spliced,
And from the lessons of that ingenious poet of yore,
A new Art of Love for our youth I have forged.[105]

Among Westerbaen's recommendations are to learn modern musical instruments such as the lute and the clavichord; he also offers advice on such things as how to entertain and how to prepare one's appearance. Many of the topics treated in Westerbaen's modernized *Avond-School* actually resemble scenes we find in paintings by Vermeer and his contemporaries. Westerbaen gives significant attention to letter writing and to the role of maids in his text. He promotes a certain amount of secrecy, though his recommendations are scrupulous in comparison with Ovid's original. Maids, first of all, need to be trustworthy in order to keep the exchange of letters secret from one's parents or guardians:

Though watched closely, you will find a way
To summon your lover by means of your maid:
You will have the chance to write to and fro:

Your letters will remain concealed, and can go.
No city is ever so guarded or secure
That no message or letter sometimes gets through.
There are many ways to write and deliver:
Your maid's bosom will not swell from any letter.
One can hide it there, or in her shoe, or her stockings,
In case one happens to make a search of her pockets.[106]

Westerbaen also devotes far more attention to the proper manner of writing than Ovid did, stressing, among other things, the importance of writing legibly, avoiding misspellings, and taking care that the hand does not appear childlike (recalling Cats's warning about "round letters").

A major figure in The Hague, just next to Delft, Westerbaen (fig. 33) worked in a milieu that revolved around the court and court culture, and his verses, often love-themed, were widely appreciated.[107] Vermeer could have easily been aware of his works. Westerbaen counted among his closest friends the diplomat and poet Constantijn Huygens (1596–1687), whose estate was down the road from his.[108] They were both highly appreciative of the arts. Westerbaen's sister, Anna, was married to the painter Salomon de Bray (1597–1664), and Westerbaen once supplied verses to a painting by his nephew Jan de Bray (1626/27–1697), celebrating the distinctly Dutch staple *paekelharing* (pickled herring).[109] While it is not possible to draw a distinct connection between Westerbaen and Vermeer, Westerbaen's love-themed editions of Ovid in the vernacular were the most popular of the day and are most likely the ones that the painter would have encountered.

Vermeer may not have known Westerbaen personally, but there appears to be a strong connection between the writer's love-themed Ovid translations and Vermeer's thematics of love and letter writing. Ovid's *Ars Amatoria* and *Heroides* likely served as distinct subtexts for love-themed genre paintings by other artists, too. Ter Borch, to name one of the most important innovators in the genre, spent most of his early career working in various courts around Europe (including London, Madrid, Brussels, and The Hague), environments in which love-themed texts such as Ovid's were perennial favorites. Early in his career, Vermeer notably abandoned history painting, the genre in which a painter would work within a highly serious and established visual tradition of depicting biblical or mythological scenes, such as his *Diana and Her Nymphs* (fig. 34), taken from Ovid's *Metamorphoses*. While the reason for his rejection of history painting from around 1657 onward has long posed a mystery, it is worth considering that we can still regard his paintings as responding in some degree to classical tradition. Ovid's love-themed texts became increasingly popular in Vermeer's day, but they still have not been fully explored in relation to love-themed genre paintings in this period. Paintings that purported to depict contemporary life could still be responsive to classical topoi, either directly or as subtext, in a way that mirrored how contemporary audiences would both read and reflect upon ancient authority to find what about it was congruous with their own lives. Love was an ancient theme, but artists like Vermeer sought to give it modern form. Like Westerbaen, he sought relevance.

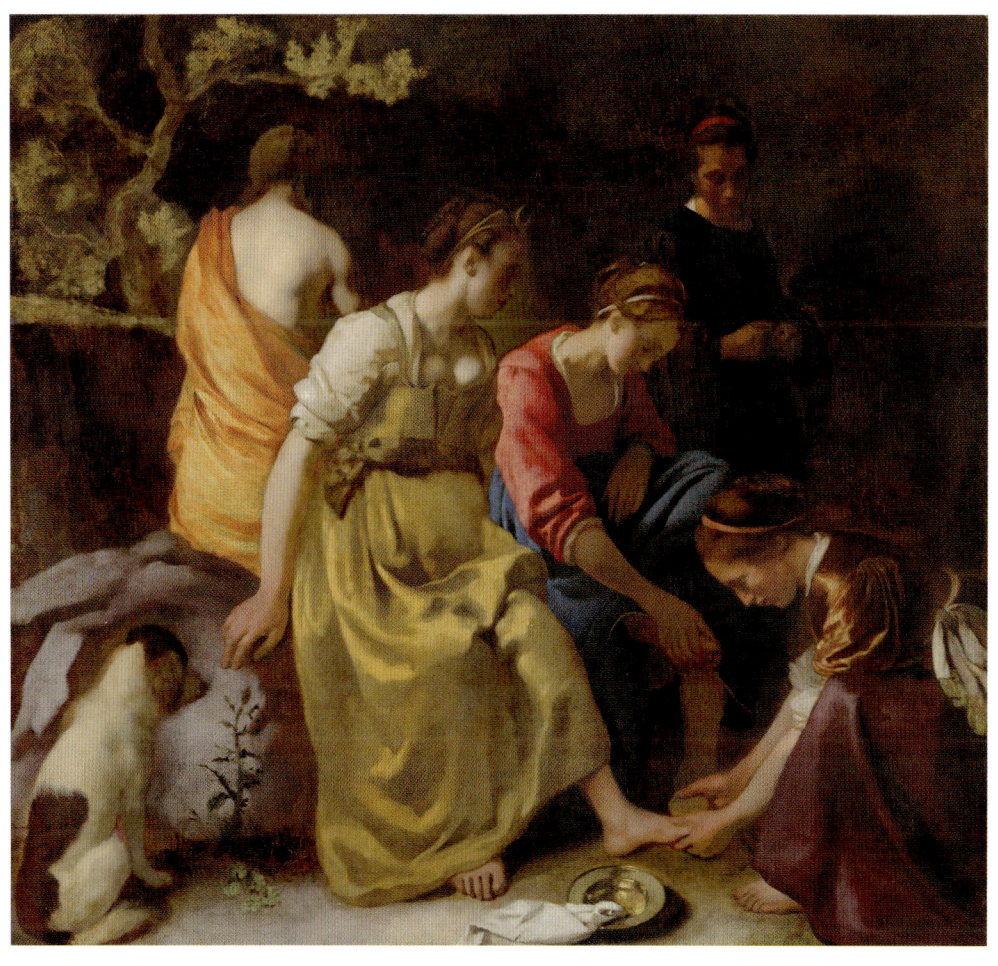

FIG. 34
Johannes Vermeer
Diana and Her Nymphs, ca. 1655–56
Oil on canvas, 38½ × 41³⁄₁₆ in. (97.8 × 104.6 cm)
Mauritshuis, The Hague

CHAPTER 4

Discretion

REFLECTING ON THE LITERATURE of the seventeenth century, the French feminist Évelyne Sullerot (1924–2017) remarked that "the passionate cries of women in love have come from men."[110] The same could be said about Dutch paintings. The development of an entire genre of art in the 1660s that focused on the subject of women in love was initiated and furthered by male artists. In this context, it is not surprising that the publication of the *Lettres d'une religieuse Portugaise* in Paris in 1669 caused a literary sensation (fig. 35).[111] In a series of letters, a Portuguese nun by the name of Marianna professes her love to an officer who had seduced and abandoned her while serving in the French army during the Portuguese Restoration War (1640–68). This unnamed cavalier, the story goes, gave these letters (a souvenir of his conquest) to a confrere in Paris, who translated them and had them published. Marianna's openheartedness, plainness of speech, passion, and outraged sense of abandonment come through in a heart-wrenching manner. In the first of five letters, she wrote (taken from a contemporary English translation):

> Your last Letter gave me such a Passion of the heart, as if it would have forced its way through my Breast, and followed you. It laid me three hours senseless: I wish it had been *dead*; for I had died of Love. But I revived: and to what end? Only to die again, and lose that Life for you, which you yourself did not think worth the saving . . . Is this your way of treating those that love you? Yet 'tis no Matter, for (do what you will)

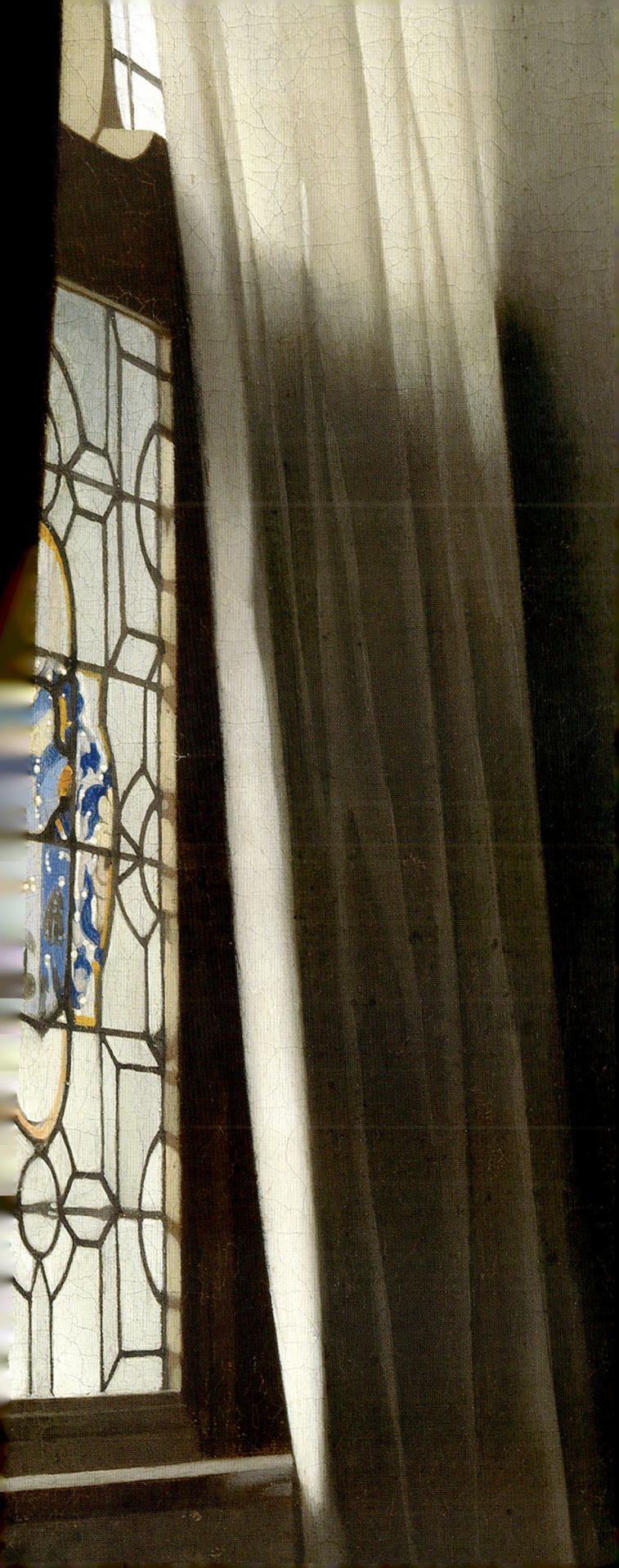

I am resolved to be firm to you to my last gasp; and never to see the Eyes of any other Mortal. And I dare assure you that it will not be the worse for you neither, if you never set your heart upon any other woman: for certainly a Passion under the degree of mine, will never content you: You may find more Beauty perhaps elsewhere (though the time was when you found no fault with mine) but you shall never meet so true a heart; and all the rest is nothing.[112]

By the last letter, Marianna has come to terms with her fate, or at least she has tried to. She wavers between despising him and wishing him no harm—and framed the affair as a harsh lesson about the vulnerability of women, especially ones who, like her, were placed in a convent at a young age. She resolves never to fall into her former "weakness" again.

It would be difficult to overstate the impact of the *Lettres Portugaises*, which was received with frenzied enthusiasm.[113] It had more than twenty documented editions and translations before 1675, with a Dutch edition already appearing in Amsterdam in 1669, within months of its initial publication.[114] It found a public weary of the type of restrained gallantry that one finds writ large in the letter-writing manuals of the day. Ovid's *Heroides* and the letters of Abelard and Heloise (which were also known at the time) offered some exposure to unrestrained female emotions around amorous love, but the *Lettres Portugaises* purported to be an actual contemporary voice for a public starving for more open expression. It was around this time that De Scudéry made her distinction between the *lettre gallante* and the *lettre d'amour*, the first staid and formal, the other tender and passionate.[115] Whether art imitated life or the other way around, it was clearly a transformative moment in the cultural history of emotional expression in Europe.

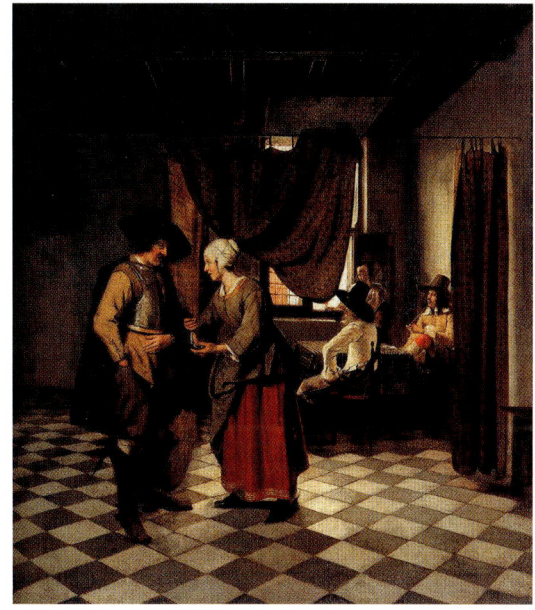

FIG. 36

Pieter de Hooch

*A Soldier Paying a Hostess
at an Inn*, 1658

Oil on canvas, 27¹⁵⁄₁₆ × 25 in.

(71 × 63.5 cm)

The Bute Collection,

Mount Stuart, Scotland

The *Lettres Portugaises* spawned an entire genre of literature. Not only did it have many imitators, but some writers "discovered" new letters, others crafted imaginative responses from the cavalier, and so forth. What began under the premise that the letters were real quickly served as a model for the reinvigorated genre of the epistolary novel. There remains a debate today whether Marianna and her cavalier were real figures or the product of the imagination of the "translator," Gabriel-Joseph de Lavergne, comte de Guilleragues (1628–1684).[116] The possibility that the count managed to impersonate a woman in the throes of love so effectively that it divides scholars today can be explained only by reference to the fact that we have virtually no contemporary models for comparison.[117] So perhaps the joke is on us; we still can be deceived by the voice of a man embodying a woman. The point, however, is that it was a man's heartless act of indiscretion in revealing these letters, real or not, that met public demand for realistic representations of women's innermost lives.

There is a remarkable frisson that Vermeer's paintings offer us in this regard. His images imply that the stakes were indeed high when it came to the act of writing and receiving love letters. He also signals the importance of discretion through the presence of maids, since they are the channel through which secrecy is maintained. The curtains featuring in all three of his letter-and-maid paintings serve a similar purpose. They thematize the inherent vulnerability of household privacy in the era. In the relatively large *Mistress and Maid* (cat. 1), the formerly green curtain (its pigment having browned) that configures the entire background compresses the space and our viewpoint with it. The maid, one imagines, has just entered the space by passing around the curtain, causing an interruption at close quarters. It allows the *juffrouw* just enough time to turn her head slightly and, taken out of her train of thought, put her hand to her chin.

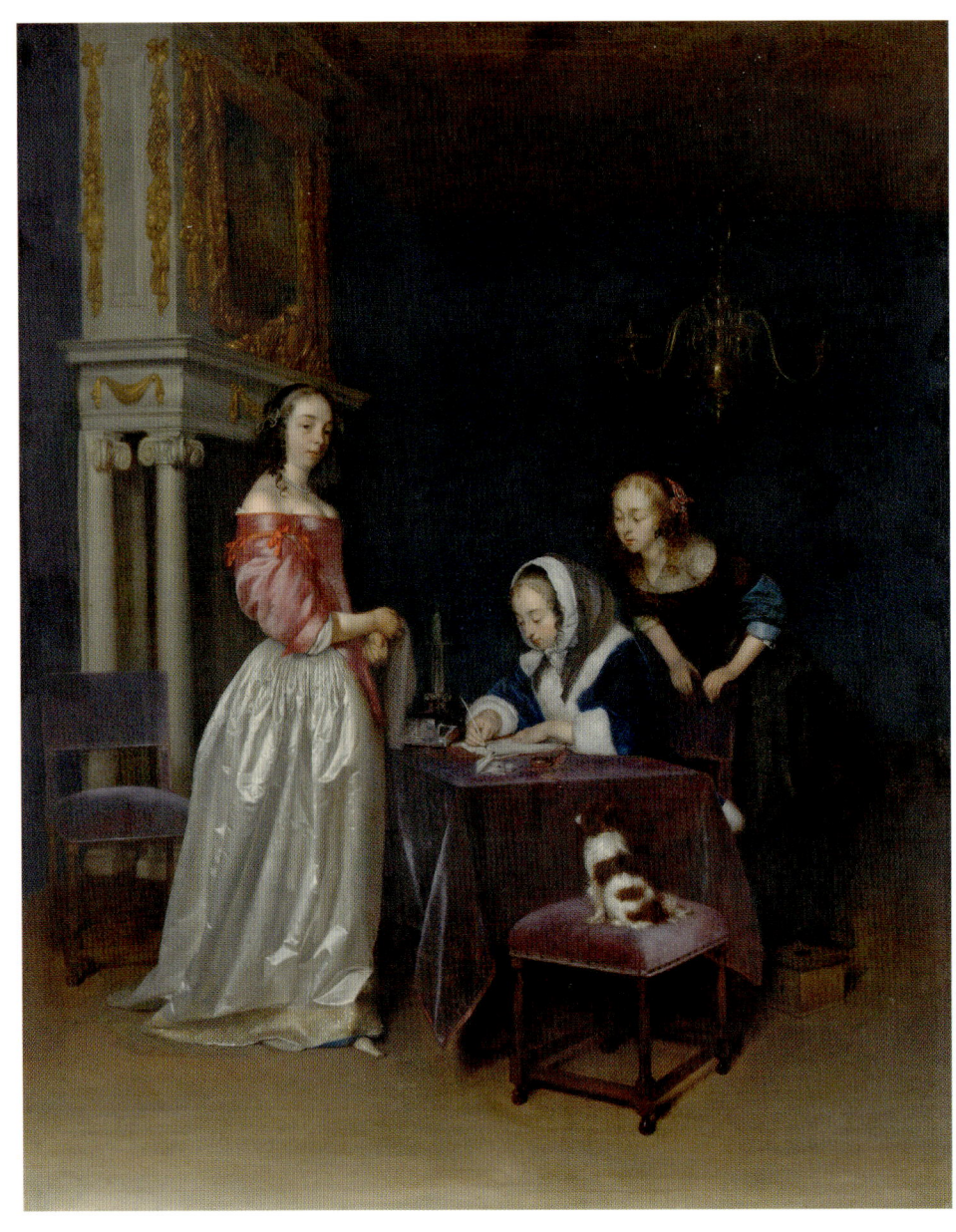

FIG. 37
Gerard ter Borch
Curiosity, ca. 1660–62
Oil on canvas, 30 × 24½ in. (76.2 × 62.2 cm)
The Metropolitan Museum of Art, New York

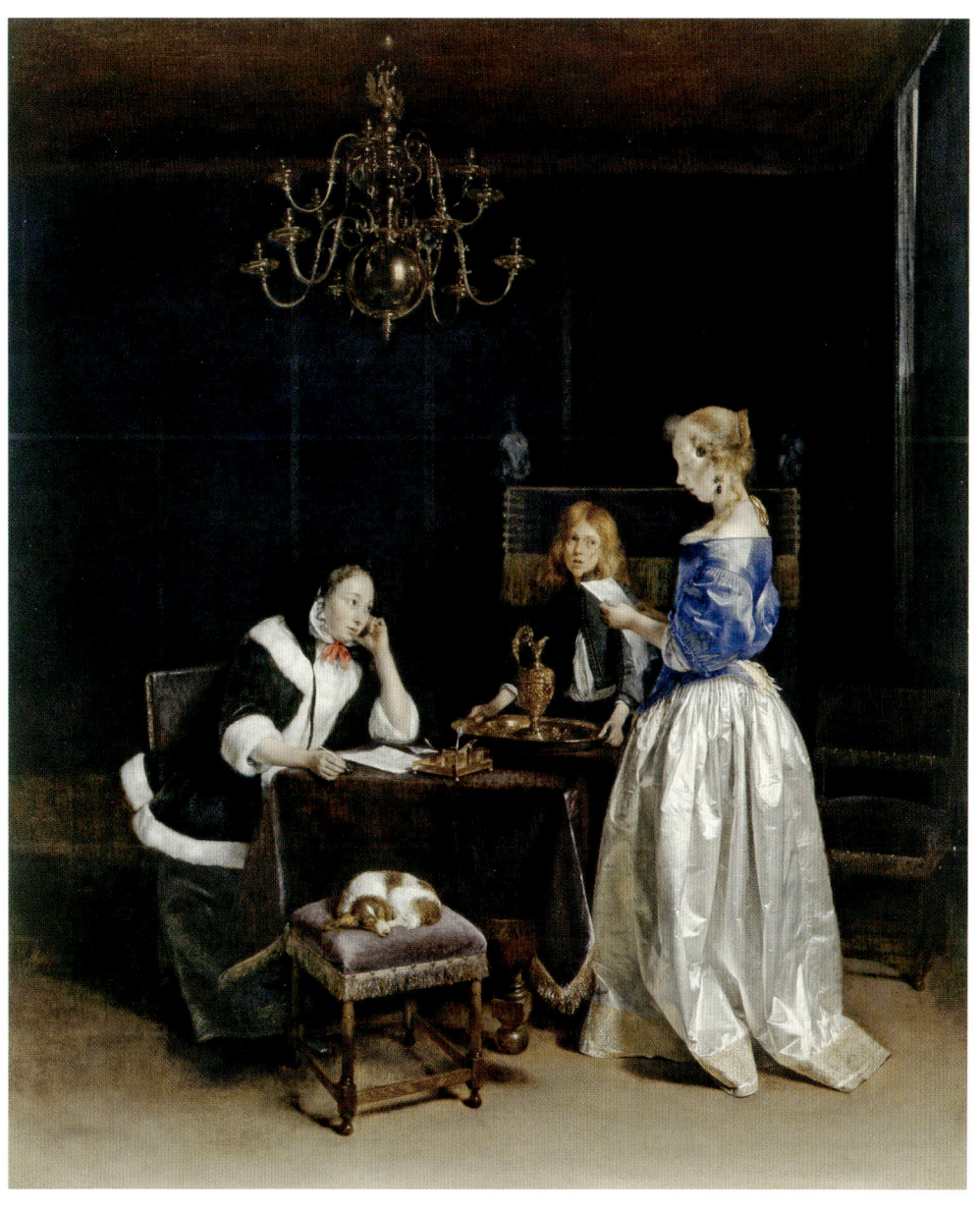

FIG. 38
Gerard ter Borch
The Letter, ca. 1660–65
Oil on canvas, 32¼ × 26¹⁵⁄₁₆ in. (81.9 × 68.4 cm)
Royal Collection Trust,
His Majesty King Charles III, Windsor

It was not unusual for curtains to function as room dividers in this period (fig. 36).[118] The relatively new phenomenon of chamberization, or the creation and use of separate rooms for distinct functions, became increasingly popular in seventeenth-century Dutch houses.[119] Curtains served to modulate spaces or to cover passages where we would normally today have an interior door.

Men, especially merchants and learned men, might have a separate office or study, then called a *comptoir* or *kantoor*, but for women this was far less common, except in the most elite households.[120] One type of woman's space was a boudoir, which may account for the canopied beds we often find in the backgrounds of genre paintings—especially those by Ter Borch—of women writing letters. In Vermeer's other two letter-and-maid paintings, we stand on the other side of a space where a curtain or tapestry serves as a nominal boundary but is pulled open. He uses it to great effect in *The Love Letter* (cat. 2), in which the open tapestry slung around a door gives us what appears to be an accidental vantage point. We might be passing through a more dimly lit space, silent and unperceived, unintentionally (or intentionally?) witnessing the delivery of a love letter. It is not happenstance that the young woman practices her cittern in a space that might be used to receive visitors, with its mantel, paintings, and red-and-gold brocaded leather wall-hanging all suggesting a relatively accessible area. Privacy for any activity in this house, the painting implies, was difficult to achieve. The room in *Woman Writing a Letter with Her Maid* (cat. 3), by contrast, offers the woman space to write, with a table affording elbow room set next to a well-lit window. Whether or not she was in a multifunctional space or in a room dedicated to study, the letter writer in this case benefits from a greater sense of light and air compared to the confined sphere of *Mistress and Maid*.[121]

Vermeer is sensitive to the effect of the viewer's position in these images. Our participation as disrupters of privacy, with whatever degree of imagination it requires, builds empathy with the figures as they undergo the often discomforting vagaries of courtship or love. By comparison, the letter-and-maid paintings by Ter Borch, such as *Curiosity* (fig. 37) and *The Letter* (fig. 38), while beautifully composed and brilliantly painted, offer a more staged viewership. In Ter Borch's paintings, we can enjoy the play of emotions without fear of intrusion, with the fourth wall (to use the term ahistorically) remaining intact. Ter Borch's "ladies in satin," as Alison Kettering notably called them, conform to the model of Petrarchan love in which women serve as objects of rapturous desire for the persistent, desperate, or forlorn men who pursue them.[122] It is a model of amorous love in which women do not emote desire any more than they do in the letter-writing manuals of the day. In fact, the underlying motif of both *Curiosity* and *The Letter* is that the love object, the woman, does not appear to be the sole author of the letter but instead has assistance in composing replies. Ter Borch was equally willing to poke fun at male counterparts doing the same (fig. 39). These figures seem to struggle with the *lettre galante*, and therein lies the humor. With a touch of the instructive but jaundiced eye of Ovid in the original *Ars Amatoria*, Ter Borch's figures attempt to master the art of seduction. In Vermeer's paintings (and in Westerbaen's *Avond-School voor Vryers en Vrysters om in de Minne-Kunst*), one gets a strong sense of a more personable approach. We cannot tell whether Vermeer's letters are *lettres galante* or *lettres d'amour*, but the moods they impart certainly suggest that the emotions involved are

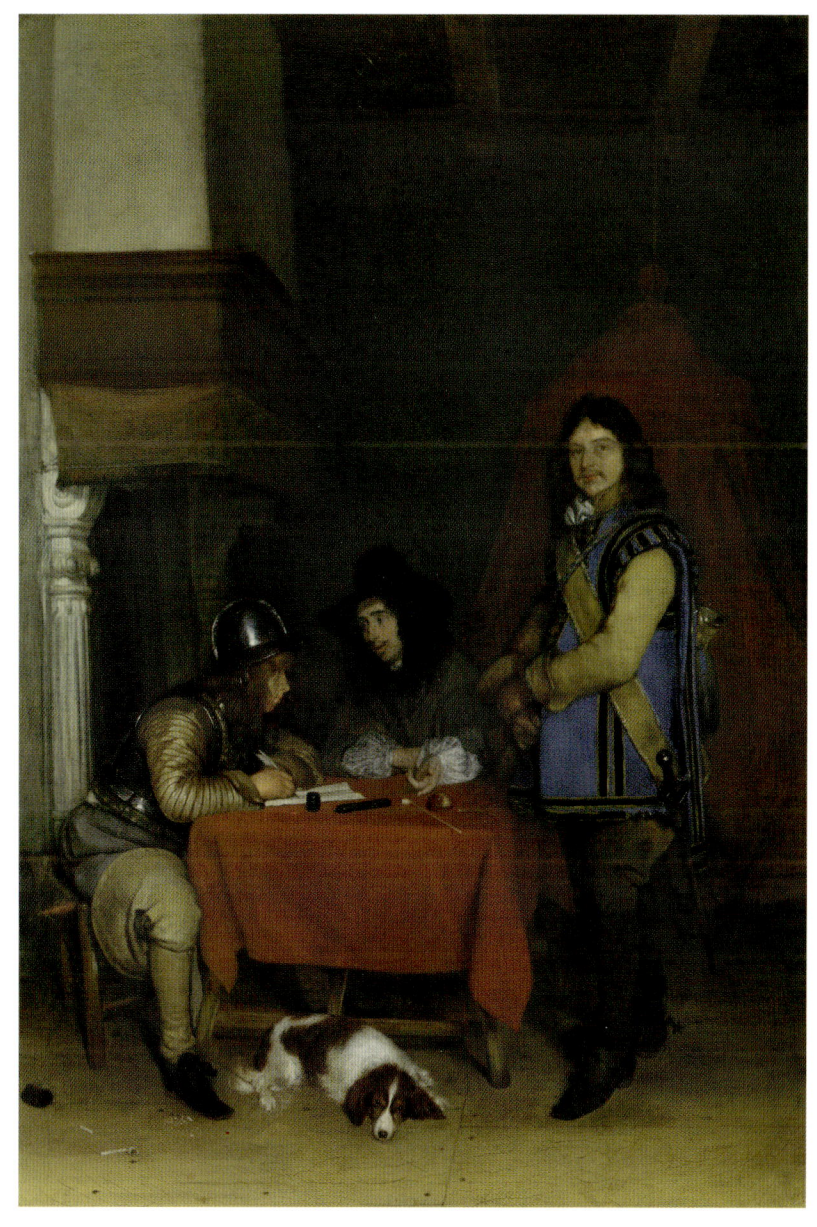

FIG. 39
Gerard ter Borch
An Officer Dictating a Letter, ca. 1655–58
Oil on canvas, 29⁵⁄₁₆ × 20¹⁄₁₆ in. (74.5 × 51 cm)
The National Gallery, London

sincere. Uncertainty, concern, or insecurity seem to mark the *Mistress and Maid* and *Love Letter* paintings, and a vigorous or at least concentrated energy permeates *Woman Writing a Letter with Her Maid*. These are female hearts that could be fulfilled or broken, and we as viewers should take them seriously.

Among the notable shifts in Dutch marriage practices at the time was the increase in love matches, what we now call romantic love. The arbitration of parents more frequently met the desires and expectations of the young couple rather than worked against them, despite whatever objections the parents might still harbor. Vermeer married Catharina Bolnes after the initial objection of her mother, with his conversion to Catholicism apparently being the deciding factor that led to her acquiescence.[123] Westerbaen also married his wife despite the objections of her family (who were of higher station).[124] It is perhaps no accident that both men specialized in love themes in their creative outputs. Whereas in 1625 Cats advised against sending letters as improper for a *vryster*, in 1665 Westerbaen gave an unambiguous nod of approval to lovers sending and receiving letters in ways that evaded the eyes of their parents. His modernized Ovid, as he makes clear, was for the young couples of his own day.

As coincidental as it might seem, one of the best visual sources we have that documents the personal interests of an actual woman from the seventeenth century is the body of art made by Ter Borch's favorite model in his genre paintings, his half-sister Gesina ter Borch. A watercolorist and painter in her own right, Gesina also assiduously collected poetry and songs, often love-themed, which she illustrated in an album now preserved in the Rijksmuseum.[125] Her chosen themes, however, still reflect the Petrarchan norms of her day: male pursuit and male desire of female love objects. Gesina's only known love interest, a merchant and amateur poet named Henrik Jordis, appears to have courted her in the late 1650s and early 1660s, but nothing ultimately came of the match, and she remained unmarried. One can only wish in vain to find in her albums more about her personal joys and sorrows in love, though there is one touching image of a woman (Gesina) carving Jordis's initials into a tree (fig. 40).[126] It would be

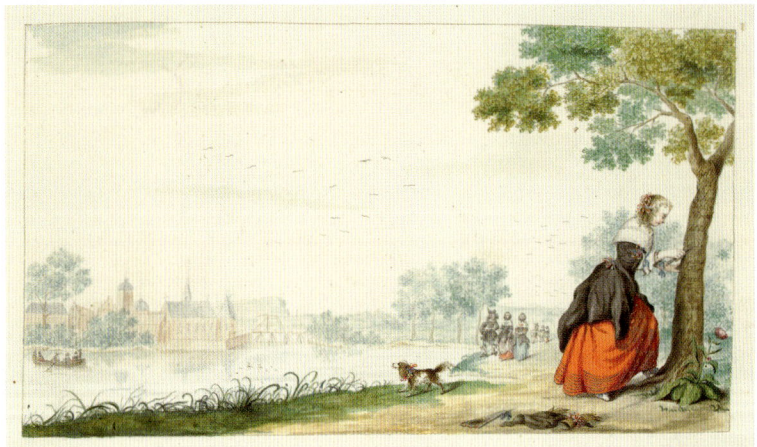

FIG. 40
Gesina ter Borch
*Self-Portrait Carving
Initials into a Tree*, 1661
Watercolor on paper,
9⁹⁄₁₆ × 14³⁄₁₆ in.
(243 × 360 mm)
Rijksmuseum,
Amsterdam

tempting to suggest that Ter Borch made use of Gesina's sorrow when he used her as a model in his paintings depicting a solitary young woman with a letter drinking wine, though of course the staging in these works points to their fictive nature (figs. 41, 42).[127] Lovesickness is also an Ovidian theme. How to handle heartbreak and rejection was precisely the concept of one of his other famous works, the *Remedia Amoris*, or the Cures for Love, which he ends with the following advice about wine:

> You ask what is my counsel concerning Bacchus' gift [i.e., wine]? Sooner than you expect you will be done with my counseling. . . . A gentle breeze fans the flame, and a strong wind kills it. Either no drunkenness at all, or so much as to banish care; anything in between is harmful.[128]

It is easy to imagine that Ter Borch and Gesina worked together on conceiving these productions, modeling love along Ovidian lines for a public receptive to such themes.[129] They nevertheless remain playful, more staged, than Vermeer's paintings.

Behind these letter-themed paintings, a well-read viewer would likely discern an authority such as Ovid, the classical writer par excellence on matters of love. One might also ask how gender factored into these paintings when the artists considered their intended or potential viewers. It has long been known that Vermeer had an important wealthy patron, or better put, patrons, in Pieter van Ruijven (1624–1674) and his wife, Maria de Knuijt (d. 1681), who collected at least twenty paintings by the artist during his lifetime.[130] Given this large number, they may have had some sort of arrangement with the artist in which they had first right of refusal. While it has often been assumed that Pieter was the driving force behind the couple's relationship with Vermeer, or at least his name alone is the one most frequently mentioned in discussions of it, art historians have recently built a good case that his wife deserves to be recognized for having much more agency in cultivating Vermeer's patronage, perhaps even more than her husband.[131] In the first place, the couple's wealth came from her side of the family. Moreover, she bequeathed 500 guilders to Vermeer in her testament in 1665, an extraordinary sum to leave someone who was not a family member.

De Knuijt and Van Ruijven certainly owned one of Vermeer's letter-and-maid paintings, as it appeared in the sale of their collection in 1696. It had passed down to their daughter, Magdalena (1655–1682), and then, after her death, to her husband, Jacob Dissius (1653–1695), a bookbinder and later a printer. The 1696 auction catalogue describes the painting as "A young lady [*juffrouw*] being brought a letter by a maid."[132] This description applies almost equally well to *Mistress and Maid* (cat. 1) and *The Love Letter* (cat. 2), but provenance research has revealed that the De Knuijt/Van Ruijven painting is almost certainly the former.[133] In this case, female patronage, and therefore female viewership, was likely considered or known from the outset.

We also know the location of one other letter-and-maid painting in the seventeenth century. On January 27, 1676, just a little more than a month after Vermeer's death, his financially pressed widow, Catharina Bolnes, transferred two paintings to their baker,

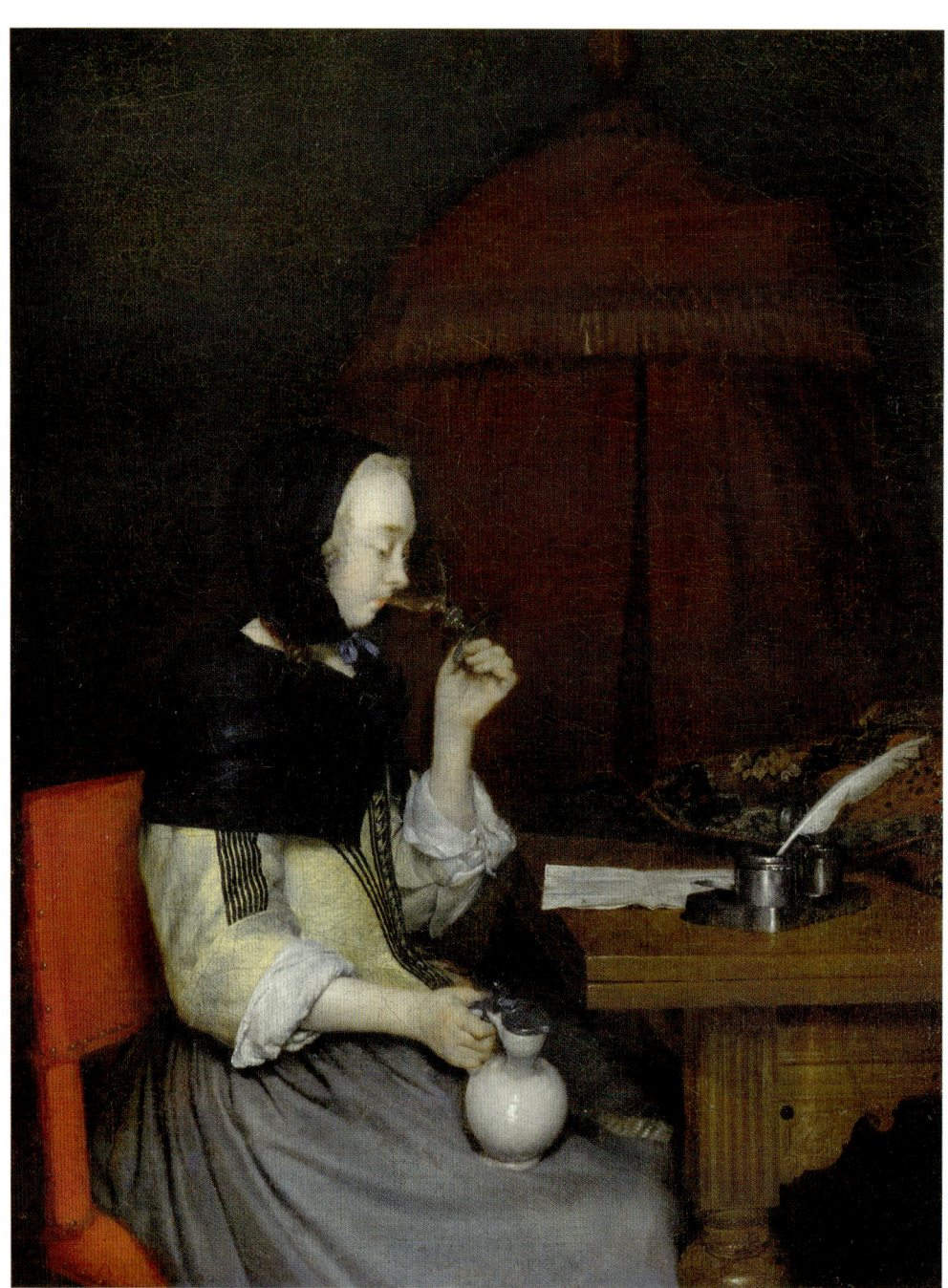

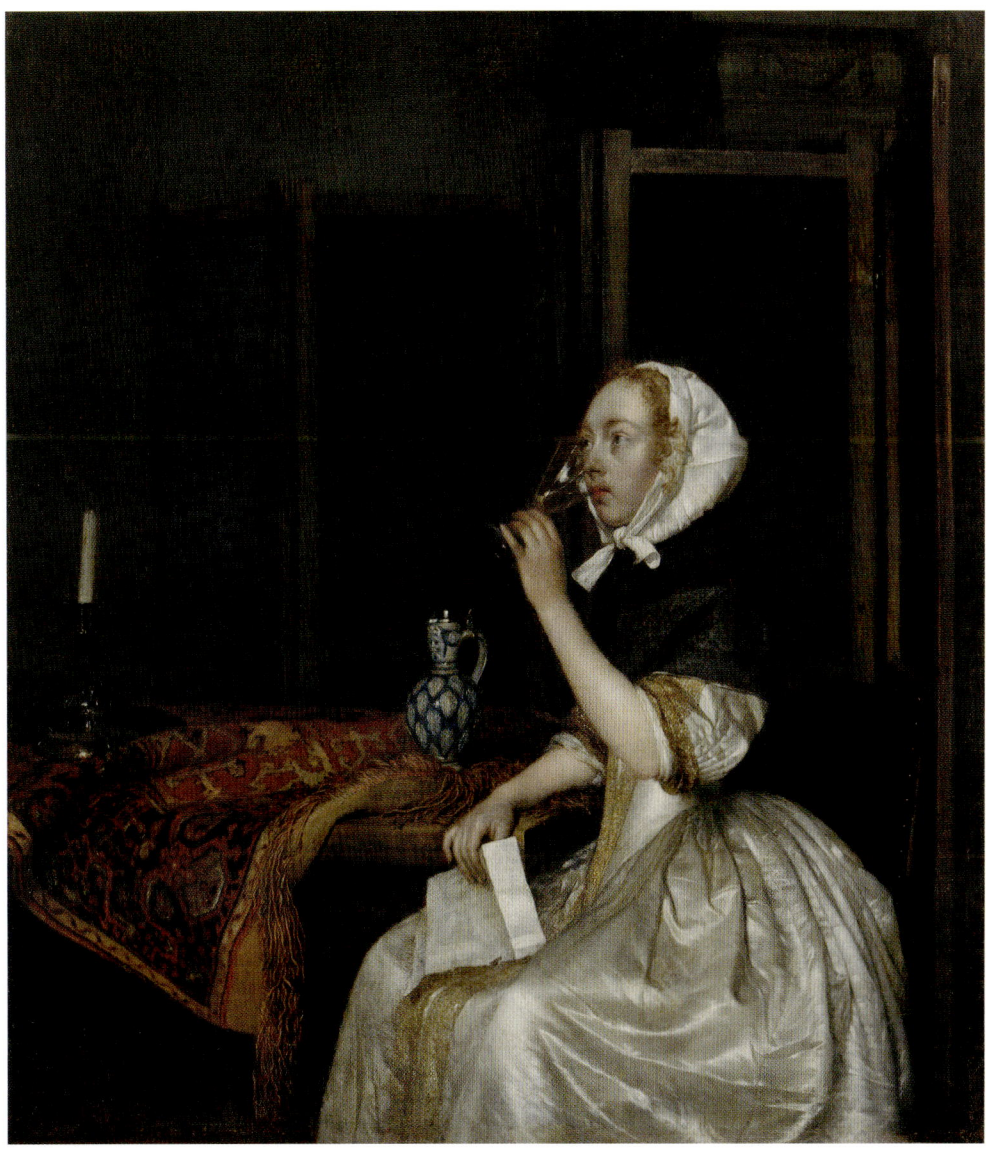

FIG. 41
Gerard ter Borch
Woman with a Wine Glass, ca. 1656–57
Oil on canvas, 14¾ × 11⁵⁄₁₆ in.
(37.5 × 28.7 cm)
Städel Museum, Frankfurt

FIG. 42
Gerard ter Borch
Woman Drinking Wine and Holding a Letter, 1665
Oil on canvas transferred from panel,
14¹⁵⁄₁₆ × 13⅜ in. (38 × 34 cm)
Sinebrychoff Art Museum, Helsinki

Hendrick van Buyten (1632–1701), in order to settle 617 guilders' worth of debt for the delivery of bread.[134] Van Buyten was markedly wealthier than most in his profession due to his business success, inheritances, and investments, and he already had at least one other work by Vermeer in his modest but impressive collection of paintings.[135] In the declaration before the notary made by Catharina and the baker, the paintings are described as "one representing two persons, one of whom is sitting writing a letter; and the other with a person playing a cittern."[136] In this case, the description of the first painting applies equally well to both *Mistress and Maid* (cat. 1) and *Woman Writing a Letter with Her Maid* (cat. 3). But since *Mistress and Maid* was presumably already in the De Knuijt/Van Ruijven collection, it must refer to the latter. Significantly, Van Buyten offered Catharina the opportunity to redeem the paintings with annual 50-guilder payments over the course of the next twelve years. This implies that these two works meant a great deal to her and that the baker, who did not charge interest in this arrangement, was sensitive to this fact. These paintings are more properly considered as belonging to Catharina, not as leftover inventory from the artist's estate.

The second painting given to Van Buyten, depicting a woman playing a cittern, has often been associated with Vermeer's *Guitar Player* (fig. 43), under the assumption that the notary mistakenly took the then newly popular guitar for the more traditional cittern. *The Guitar Player*, however, was almost certainly in the De Knuijt/Van Ruijven collection at the time since it appeared in the 1696 Dissius auction. We can also be fairly certain that Catharina would know the difference between a guitar and a cittern. This was not a case of an inventory-taker quickly walking through a house making notes but rather a record of a detailed arrangement for which Catharina would have been present and perhaps would even have provided descriptions of the paintings. There remains only one painting by Vermeer that depicts a woman playing a cittern, and that is *The Love Letter* (cat. 2). Although it has not been suggested before, it may also have been in Caterina's possession at the time of the artist's death. If so, she held on to not just one but two of Vermeer's love-letter paintings, both featuring a maid. In the end, whether one or both belonged to her, neither of these cherished works revolving around the expression of love through the exchange of letters, glances, and knowing smiles, appears to have made its way back into her hands.

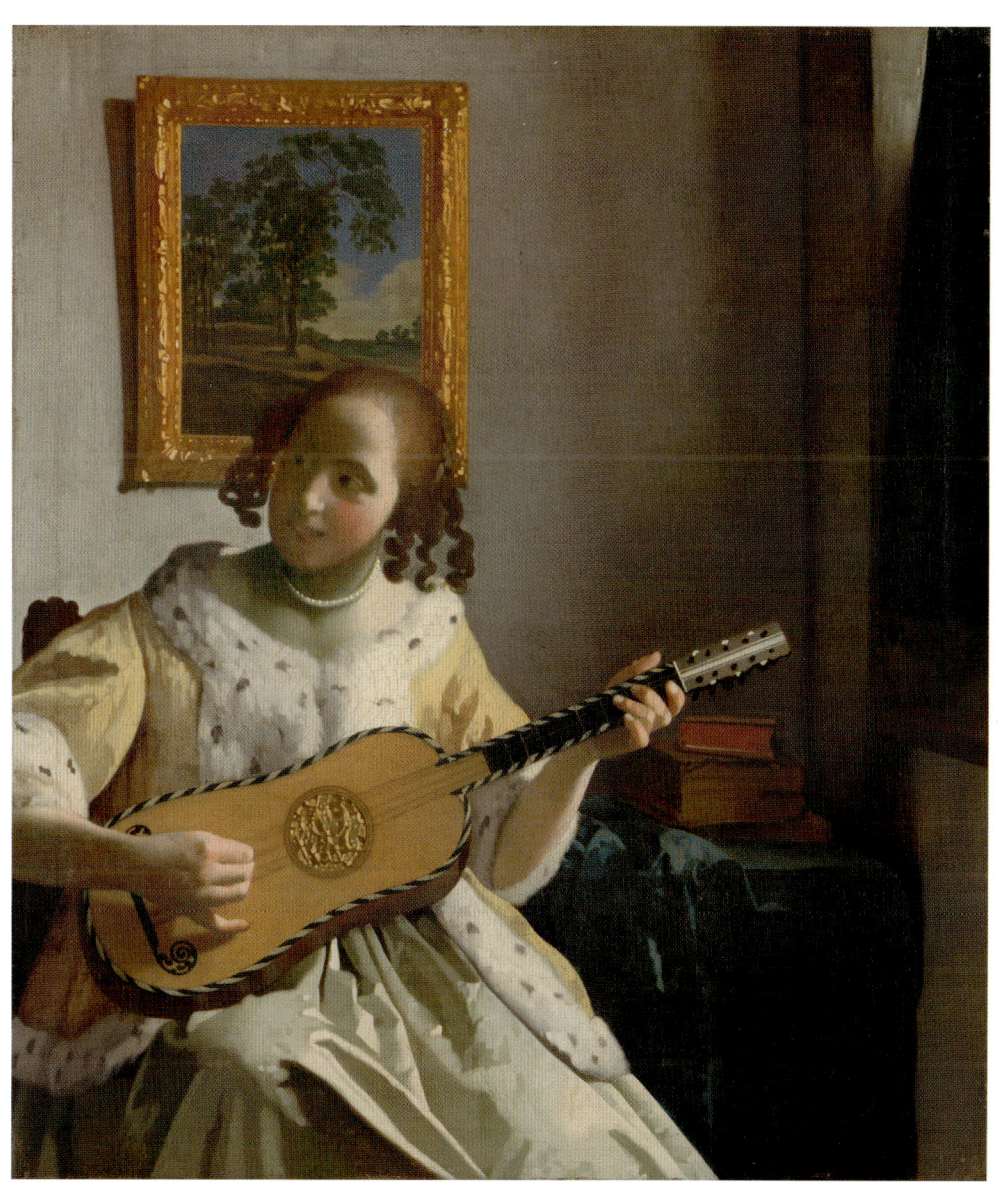

FIG. 43
Johannes Vermeer
The Guitar Player, ca. 1670–72
Oil on canvas, 20¼ × 17¾ in. (51.4 × 45.1 cm)
Kenwood, London

79

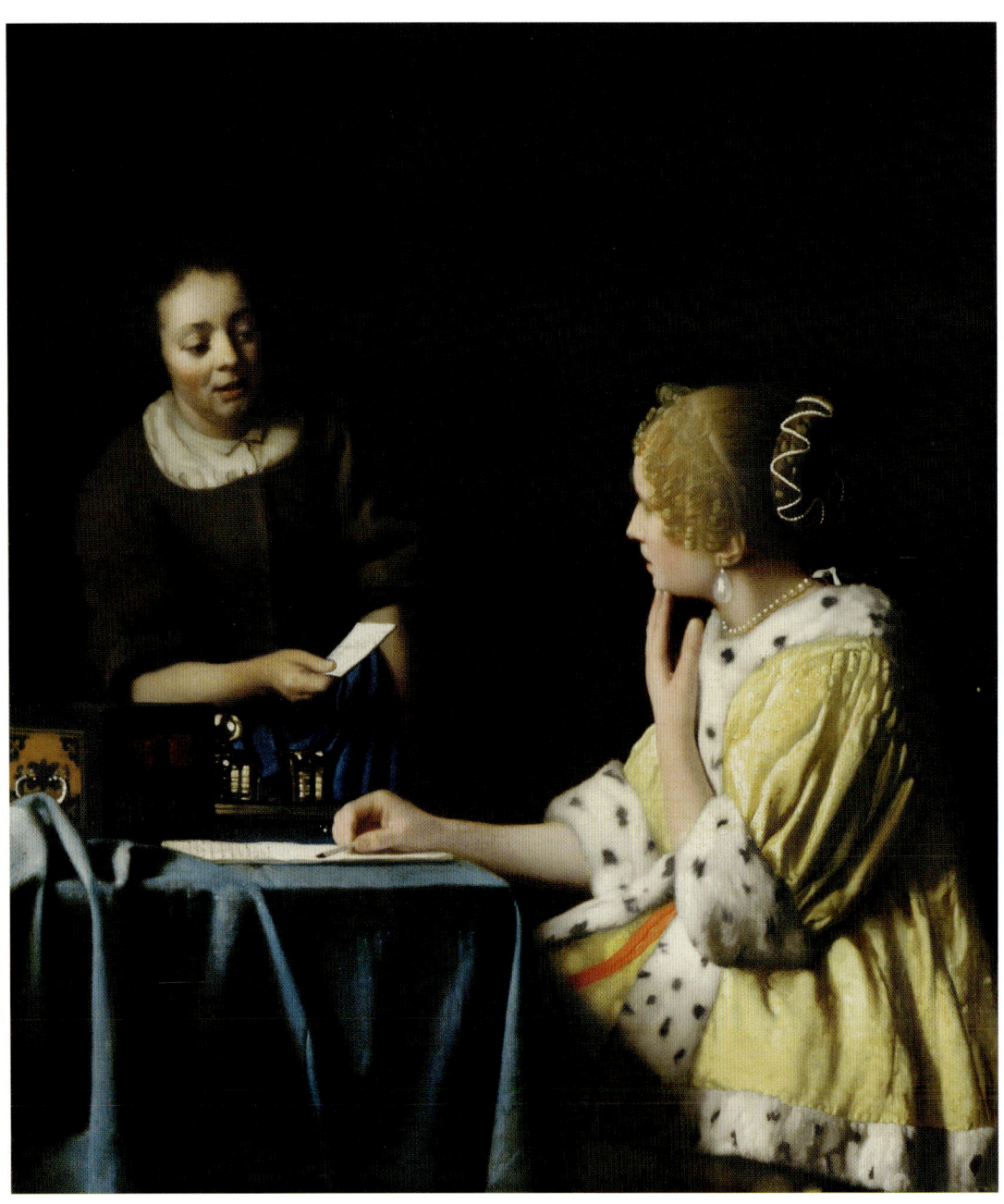

CAT. 1

Johannes Vermeer
Mistress and Maid, ca. 1664–67
Oil on canvas, 35½ × 31 in. (90.2 × 78.7 cm)
The Frick Collection, New York

PROVENANCE:
Maria Simonsdr de Knuijt (1623–1681) and Pieter Claesz. van Ruijven (1624–1674), Delft; their daughter, Magdalena van Ruijven (1655–1682), Delft; her widower, Jacob Dissius (1653–1695), Delft; his sale, Amsterdam, May 16, 1696, no. 7, fl. 70; likely acquired at the sale by Jacob Oortman (1661–1738), Amsterdam; his sale, Amsterdam (Haring), October 15, 1738, no. 12, fl. 160, to Hendrik Oortman (1696–1748), Amsterdam; his sale, Amsterdam, January 9, 1749, no. 6; sale, Helsleuter et al., Paris (A. Paillet and H. Delaroche), January 25, 1802, no. 106 (bought in at fr. 2,000). Sale, Auguste-Louis-Cesar-Hyppolite-Theodore de L'Espinasse de Langeac (1749–1814), Paris (A. Paillet and H. Delaroche), January 16, 1809, no. 84, fr. 600, to C. Lebrun; his sale, Paris, March 20 (22), 1810, no. 143, fr. 601, to Chevallier. Sale, Drouillet and De Bertinval, Paris (Paillet), March 24, 1818, no. 48, fr. 460. Collection Dufour, Marseilles. Sale, Marie-Caroline of Bourbon-Two Sicilies, Duchess of Berry (1798–1870), Paris (Bataillard), April 4, 1837, no. 76, fr. 4,015, to Paillet. Sale, Eugène Secrétan (1836–1899), Paris (Broussod et al.), July 1, 1889, no. 139, fr. 75,000, to dealer Charles Sedelmeyer; Alexander Polovstov, St. Petersburg. Lawrie & Co., London. Dealer Sulley & Co., London, 1905; by whom sold to dealer M. Knoedler & Co., 1905; by whom sold to dealer Sulley & Co., London, 1906; from whom purchased for DM 325,000 by James Simon (1851–1932), Berlin, 1906; by whom sold to dealer A. Preyer for Henry Clay Frick (1849–1919), New York, 1919; transferred to The Frick Collection, New York.

SELECTED LITERATURE:
Blankert 1978, no. 21 (ca. 1666–67); Nash 1991, 84–85; Wheelock 1995, 140–47 (ca. 1667–68); Liedtke 2000, 239–42; Vergara 2003; Liedtke 2008, no. 21 (ca. 1666–67); Franits 2015, 236–41 (ca. 1667–68); Iacono 2018; Wieseman 2023; Amsterdam 2023, no. 22 (ca. 1664–67).

81

A NOTABLE ASPECT OF THIS PAINTING is its large size, at least compared to most from Vermeer's mature career, and the fact that the figures approach a life-size scale. The lowered viewpoint and the figures' proximity to the picture plane bind our line of sight to that of the young woman being handed the letter. The maid's arm extends into our space as much as hers. The overall effect concentrates our attention on the focus of the image: the arrival of the letter and the anticipatory moment when the contents of a message are about to be revealed. The key gesture of response by the woman receiving the letter is that she puts her hand to her chin. She does so with the gentlest of touches, perfectly registering a sense of inquisitiveness combined perhaps with slight concern. Her searching gaze does not rest on the letter but rather on the maid, who appears to be speaking. Just as the letter remains sealed, Vermeer leaves us equally in the dark when we try to decipher the maid's expression in visual terms alone. An ingeniously subtle detail is the position of the quill pen in the woman's other hand. She holds it at the far end with the inked nub just hovering over the surface of the paper. Her grip is not one of writing but of thinking. She appears to have been searching for words before being interrupted by the maid.

The once-green curtain that forms the backdrop of the painting has darkened over time, making it difficult to have a sense of the original color balance between foreground and background, leading the figures to emerge from darkness with an almost Caravaggesque gravitas.[137] The curtain nevertheless once functioned to compress the space and to emphasize the privacy of the interaction.[138] Curtains often served as room dividers in Dutch houses, or to cover interior doorways or passageways, and could be opened or closed according to the needs of privacy. Emphasizing its closed-off nature, an auction catalogue entry from 1738 described this painting as "a writing *juffertje* in her inner chamber [*binnenkamer*] who receives a letter."[139] Private space could be created when needed in this period when a separate office space or study, especially for women, was quite rare. Technical research has revealed that Vermeer originally painted a tapestry as a backdrop instead of a curtain, one that was decorated with a pattern or perhaps contained a narrative scene (fig. 44).[140] He may have found that the patterning of the tapestry interfered too much with the foreground figures and opted for a curtain instead. On other occasions, however, Vermeer did choose to use a tapestry backdrop, as in *Girl with a Red Hat* and *Girl with a Flute*, both in the National Gallery of Art, Washington. A more recent technical study has also revealed that Vermeer's *Girl with a Pearl Earring* once had a green curtain in the background (fig. 45).[141] Its curtain has also darkened considerably (in this case to the point of near invisibility) but reveals an unexpected link with the Frick's *Mistress and Maid*, which dates to the same years.

Another link between these two paintings is the pearl earring, as large and prominently depicted as those found in any of Vermeer's works. The actual object was likely made of glass (since real ones were smaller and exorbitantly priced), probably from Venice, where artisans

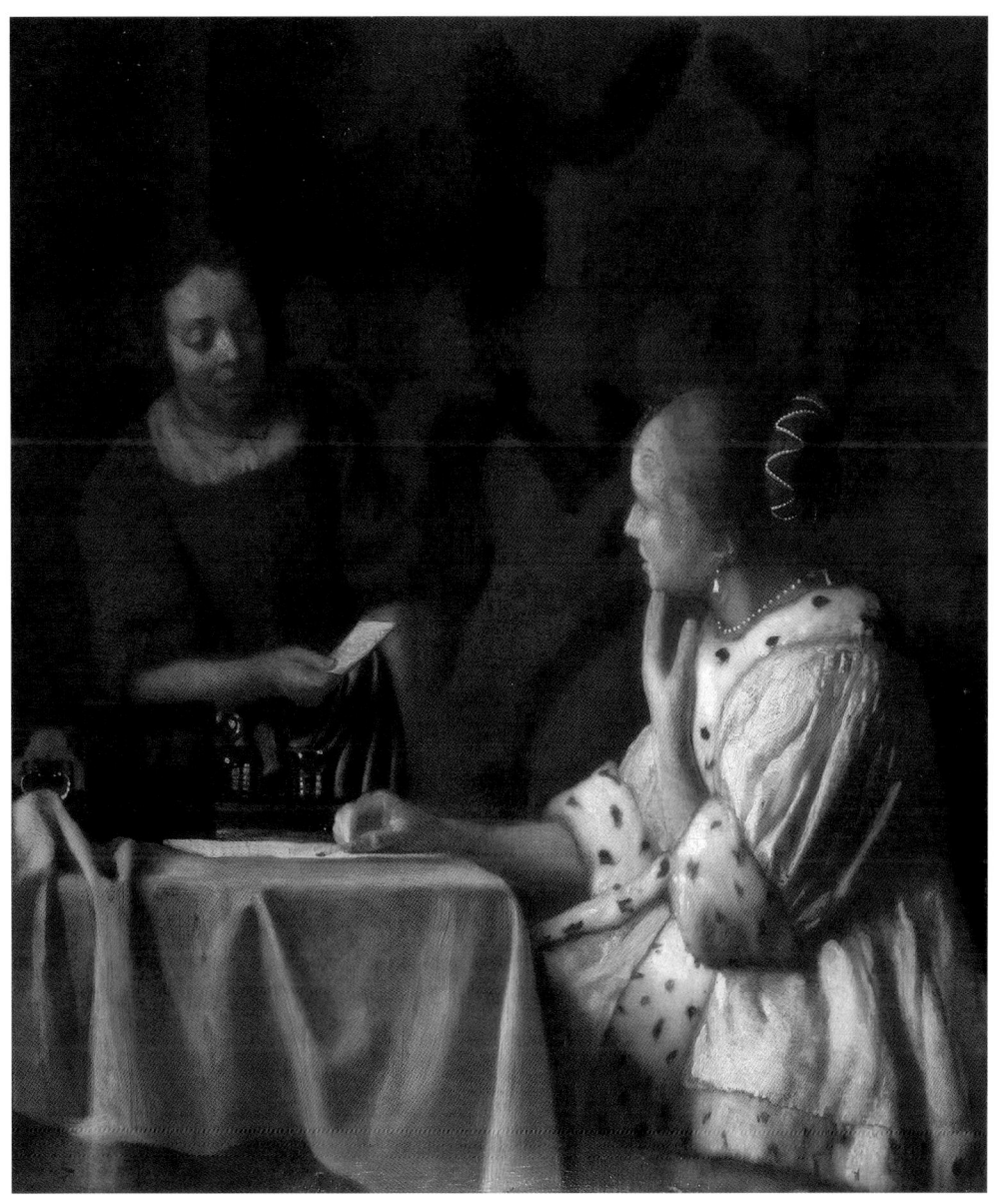

FIG. 44
Infrared reflectography image of
Mistress and Maid

specialized in imitation pearls.[142] Another item in this painting found in the artist's other works is the fur-trimmed yellow mantle, which appears in five other paintings.[143] The wooden coffer with inlaid decorations (often described as a jewelry box but which may also contain letters) appears to be a product from India, having reached Europe via trade with Goa.[144] Both the inkstand and the coffer also appear in *A Lady Writing* (see fig. 11), likewise sitting on a table with a blue tablecloth, a painting assumed to have been made around the same time given its similar subject matter and style.[145]

This painting was once considered unfinished due to its softer articulation of form and less-precise brushstrokes, but more recent scholarship has related its appearance to intentional artistic strategies Vermeer undertook that are in keeping with his exploration of optical effects in related works.[146] The edges of the figures and objects in this painting would probably have been more legible against the background when the curtain was more defined and colorful. In any case, Vermeer's touch in this work stands at a remove from some of his other, more precisely rendered, love-letter paintings. The staging of the figures so close to the picture plane also appears experimental, offering the viewer a more direct engagement with the subject. In that sense, it resembles Caravaggist paintings from the previous generation, with which Vermeer was quite familiar.

When this painting first appeared at auction in 1696, it was described as "a *juffrouw* being brought a letter by a maid," and it sold for the respectable sum of 70 guilders.[147] Its appearance in this sale reflects the fact that it once belonged to Vermeer's primary patrons, Maria de Knuijt and Pieter van Ruijven. Given its scale, it was possibly commissioned by them. The suggestion that it may have been designed to hang high (perhaps as part of a mantelpiece) due to its size and lowered viewpoint does not seem convincing, as its more effectual elements are better viewed at eye level.[148] Many years later, in 1864, during one of the moments it became available for purchase, the director of the National Gallery, London, dismissed the work as one that was a "familiar, unimportant scene," repeating the then-popular cliché about the prosaic nature of Dutch art.[149] Grounded more properly in its cultural milieu, however, this dynamic painting bears witness to the range of dramatic associations that courtship and love-related themes offered painters at the time, and that their publics found so appealing.

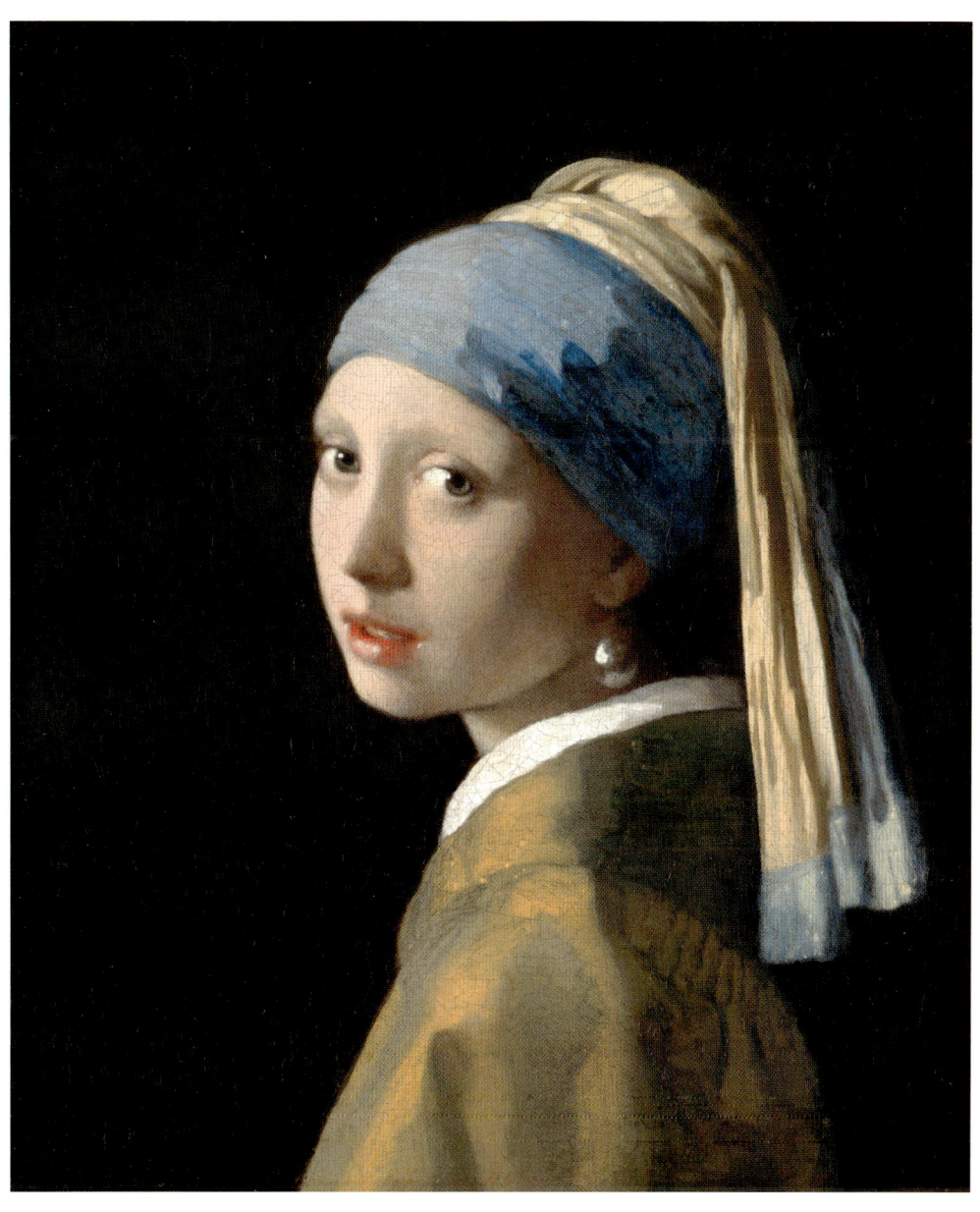

FIG. 45
Johannes Vermeer
Girl with a Pearl Earring, ca. 1664–67
Oil on canvas, 17½ × 15⅜ in. (44.5 × 39 cm)
Mauritshuis, The Hague

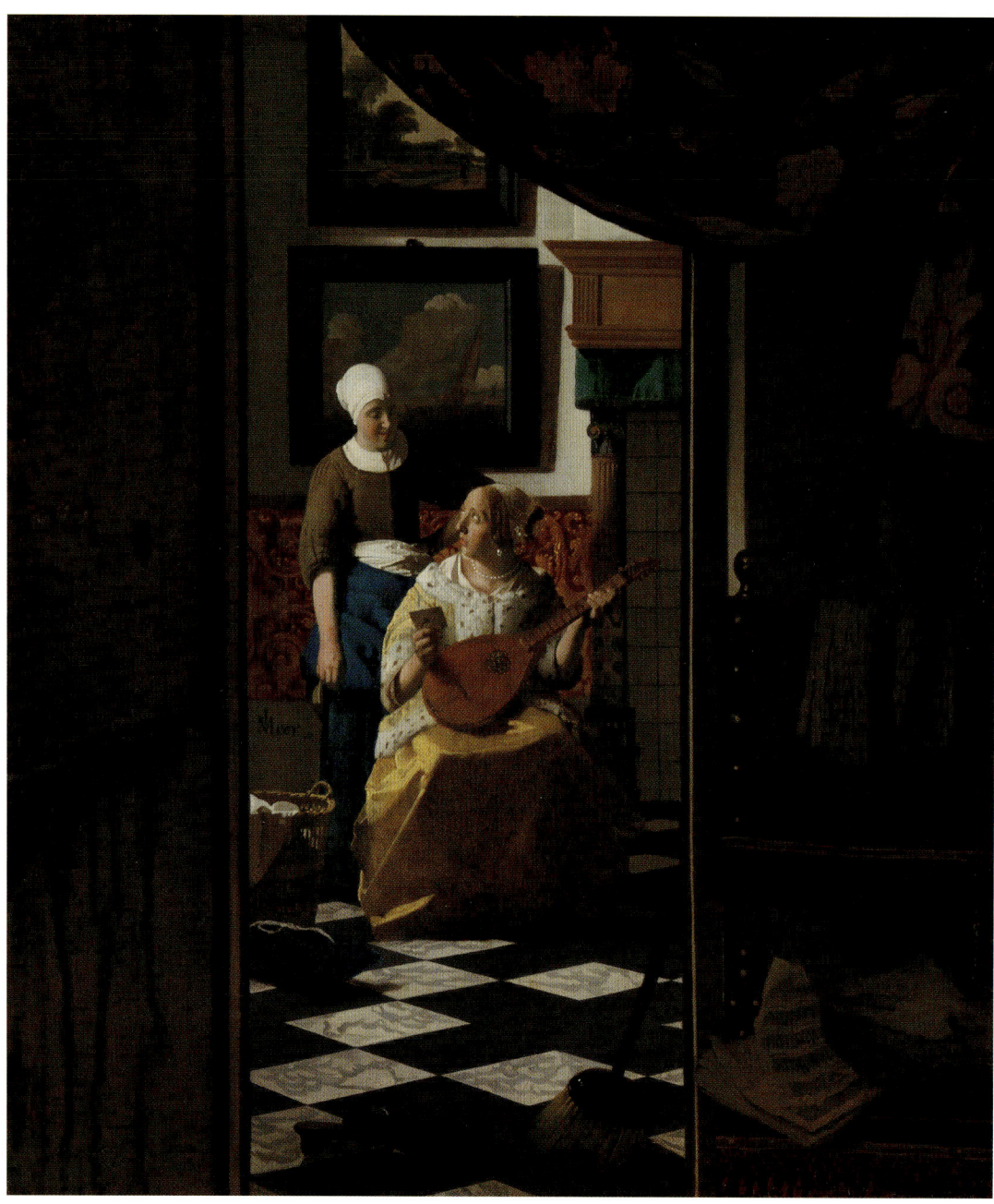

CAT. 2

Johannes Vermeer
The Love Letter, ca. 1669–70
Oil on canvas, 17⁵⁄₁₆ × 15³⁄₁₆ in. (44 × 38.5 cm)
Signed on the back wall:
IVMeer (the first three letters in ligature)
Rijksmuseum, Amsterdam

PROVENANCE:
Possibly Catharina Bolnes (ca. 1631–1687), Vermeer's widow, Delft; possibly transferred in 1676 to Hendrick van
Buyten (1632–1701), Delft, as collateral to settle a debt; Pieter van Lennep (1780–1850), Amsterdam; his daughter,
Margaretha Catharina Messchert van Vollenhoven-Van Lennep (1815–1891), Bloemendaal; in inheritance to J. F. van
Lennep (1819–1892), Amsterdam; sale, Messchert van Vollenhoven and Van Engelenberg, Amsterdam (C. F. Roos),
March 29, 1892, no. 14, fl. 41,000, to J. Ankersmit of the Rembrandt Association for the Rijksmuseum, Amsterdam.

SELECTED LITERATURE:
Blankert 1978, no. 22 (ca. 1667); Nash 1991, 82–83; Washington and The Hague 1995–96, no. 18 (ca. 1669–70);
Dublin and Greenwich 2003–4, no. 38 bis (ca. 1667–70); Vergara 2003; Liedtke 2008, no. 30 (ca. 1669–70); Franits
2015, 208–9 (ca. 1668–69); Paris, Dublin, and Washington 2017–18, no. 21.3 (ca. 1669–70); Landsman 2022, 88–91,
107–8; Wieseman 2023; Amsterdam 2023, no. 31 (ca. 1669–70).

IN THIS WORK, VERMEER COMBINES two of his most distinctive themes: letters and music. Before the maid's arrival, the seated woman was practicing on a cittern, a then-popular stringed instrument that has a thinner body than a lute and uses metal strings instead of gut to create a loud, resonant sound.[150] Vermeer frequently depicted young women playing music, either alone or in the company of men. Only in one other painting, *Young Woman with a Lute*, is it clear that she is practicing rather than performing, since she is tuning her instrument while looking out the window (fig. 46). Two other citterns appear in Vermeer's oeuvre, though they are not being played but instead are resting on furniture—on the chair in *Glass of Wine* (Gemäldegalerie, Staatliche Museen zu Berlin) and on the table in *Girl Interrupted at Her Music* (fig. 47). Because music making was such an essential aspect of courtship, the meaning of Vermeer's women who practice their instruments revolves around the expectation or hope of a future duet, which is what makes the delivery of the letter doubly apropos in this context of the theme of anticipation.[151]

As with *Mistress and Maid*, the exchange of glances between the *juffrouw* and the maid defines this particular moment within a larger, unknown narrative. In this case, a clear smile has formed on the maid's face, seemingly by way of reassurance, and her hand on her hip also might express a satisfied (or see-I-told-you-so) outcome. The look of uncertainty on the young woman's face, as well as her seated position (forcing her to look up), seems to suggest that she is under the maid's power and dependent on her to act as a go-between for the exchange of letters. The artist may have intended a slight touch of humor in this exchange, despite our natural inclination to take Vermeer quite seriously as we probe his images for meaning. One important and at least outwardly obvious clue as to the nature of this courtship can be found in the fair-weather seascape hanging behind them. In the Dutch emblem-book literature of the time, such an image can be a token of a love affair that is sailing smoothly.[152] It appears to be one of the clearest painting-within-a-painting metaphors in Vermeer's oeuvre, deployed to dispel doubts about the *juffrouw*'s prospects as mirrored by the expression and pose of the maid.

One of the most notable features of the painting is its ambitious perspectival construction, which affords us a deep view through a doorway.[153] The main scene takes place in a room that is disconnected and distant from the viewer's position, with the central episode filling less than half of the canvas's surface area in one vertical strip through the middle.[154] Aside from an artistic desire to use a highly innovative point of view, the strategy of nearly removing us from the scene paradoxically fastens us to it more closely by making us unnoticed participants in a private exchange. We are given a role in the work, though Vermeer leaves open the question of whether we stand there on purpose or not. Our gaze might be accidental (if just passing by) or furtive (if we are spying). The objects that clutter the foreground do not distract our view because they are in shadow, reinforcing our hidden vantage point as a viewer. On the right, crumpled sheet music sits awkwardly on a chair, with a scarf or shawl slung casually over it. Before us we find discarded

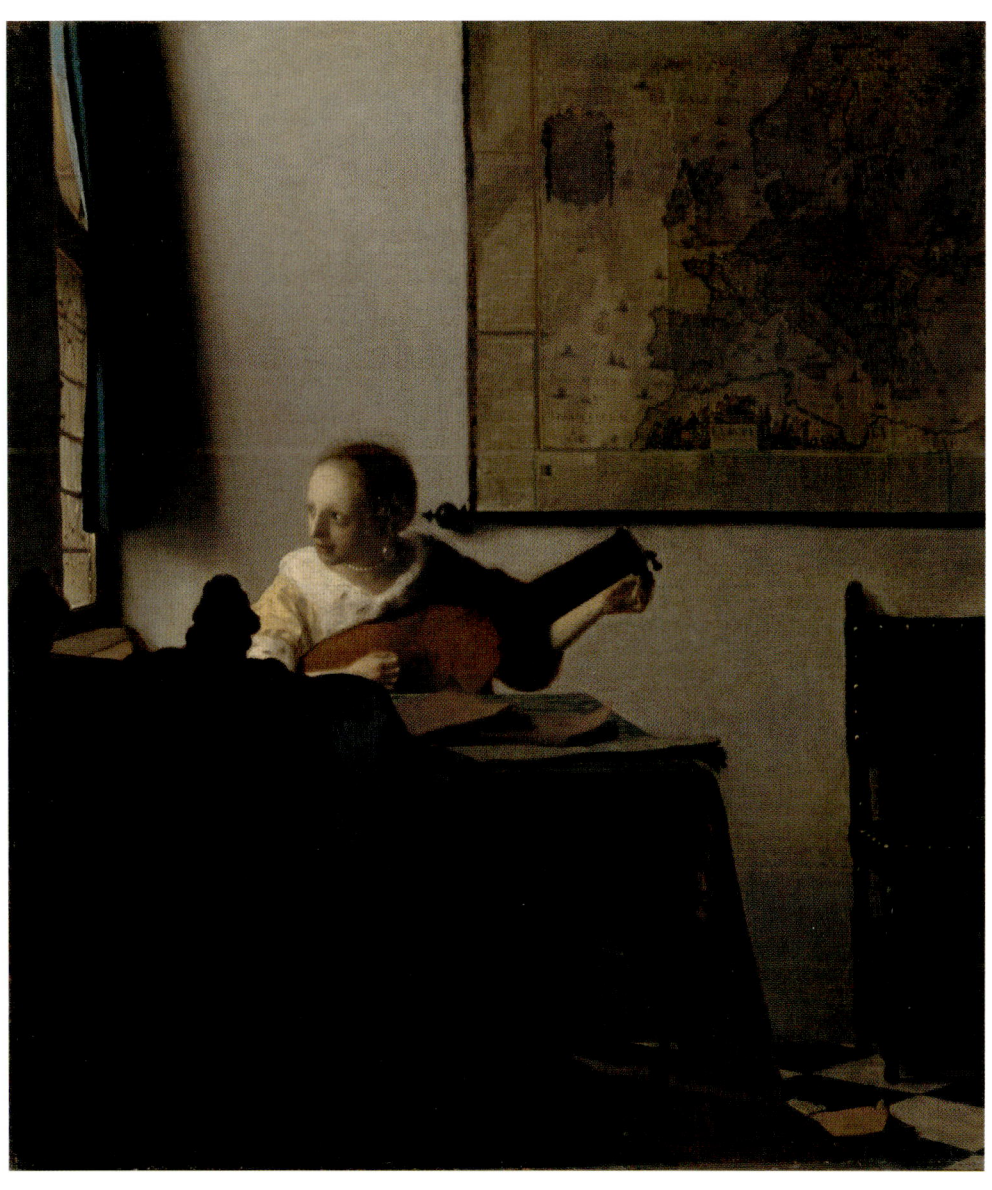

FIG. 46
Johannes Vermeer
Young Woman with a Lute, ca. 1662–64
Oil on canvas, 20¼ × 18 in. (51.4 × 45.7 cm)
The Metropolitan Museum of Art, New York

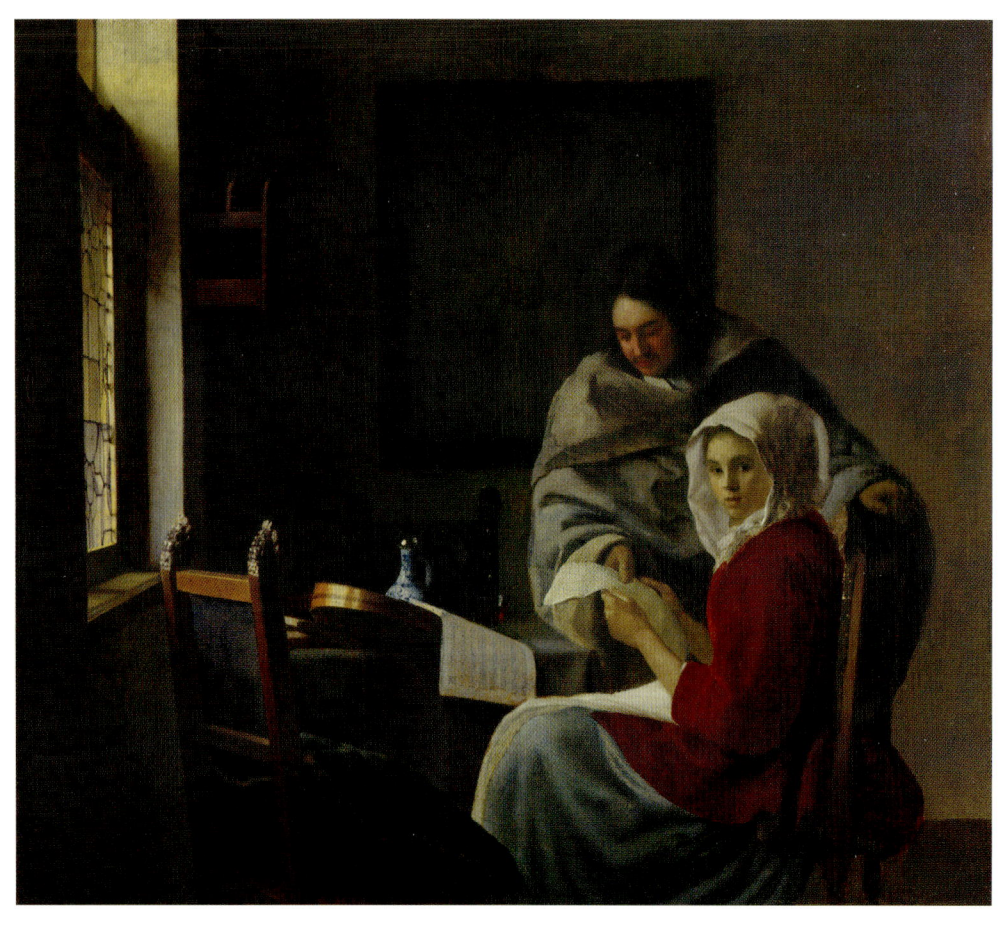

FIG. 47

Johannes Vermeer

Girl Interrupted at Her Music, ca. 1659–61

Oil on canvas, 15½ × 17½ in. (39.4 × 44.5 cm)

The Frick Collection, New York

clogs and a broom and, beyond them, a linen basket and sewing cushion.[155] To the left, a map of Holland and West Friesland (also found in two other works by Vermeer) hangs on a wall.[156] The prominent streaky stains beneath the map, so antithetical to the artist's otherwise perfectly appointed interiors, underpin the notion that we stand in a passageway or storage space, not in a room that would normally serve the purposes of public occupation and polite conversation.

The early provenance of the painting has long been a mystery. Its first and only known appearance on the market was in 1892, when the Rijksmuseum acquired it with the assistance of the Rembrandt Association.[157] It had been in the Messchert van Vollenhoven family for at least two or three generations. At first glance, it appears to match a description of one of the paintings in the 1696 auction of the collection formed by Vermeer's main patrons, Maria de Knuijt and Pieter van Ruijven, catalogued as "a *juffrouw* being brought a letter by a maid."[158] This work, however, is now understood through further provenance research to be the painting in The Frick Collection, which fits the same description (cat. 1). As discussed in Chapter Four, an idea presented here is that *The Love Letter* was one of the two paintings that Vermeer's widow, Catharina Bolnes, transferred to the baker Hendrick van Buyten just weeks after the artist's death in order to settle a large debt. The description of the two paintings in the 1676 transaction before the notary reads, "one representing two persons, one of whom is sitting writing a letter; and the other with a person playing a cittern."[159] The first painting was more likely *Woman Writing a Letter with Her Maid* (cat. 3) rather than the Frick's *Mistress and Maid*, though they both fit the description.[160] The second one, however, was long thought to represent Vermeer's *Guitar Player* at Kenwood (see fig. 43), under the assumption that the notary had misidentified the instrument. This old theory is no longer tenable as we now know that that painting was already in the De Knuijt/Van Ruijven collection.[161] It is also highly probable that Catharina (if not the notary) would have known the difference between a cittern and a guitar. *The Love Letter* is the only painting in Vermeer's oeuvre that fits the description of a person playing a cittern noted in the exchange with the baker, and the letter theme would have been in keeping with the other painting she exchanged with him. Some of the works that Catharina held at the time of Vermeer's death were likely personal possessions of the couple, not intended for sale. We can at least be certain that the two paintings she transferred to the baker were dear to her. Due to Catharina's pleading, the document notes, Van Buyten kindly offered her the chance to redeem the paintings if she managed to pay back the debt in annual installments, something she was probably unable to do, given her later financial constraints.[162]

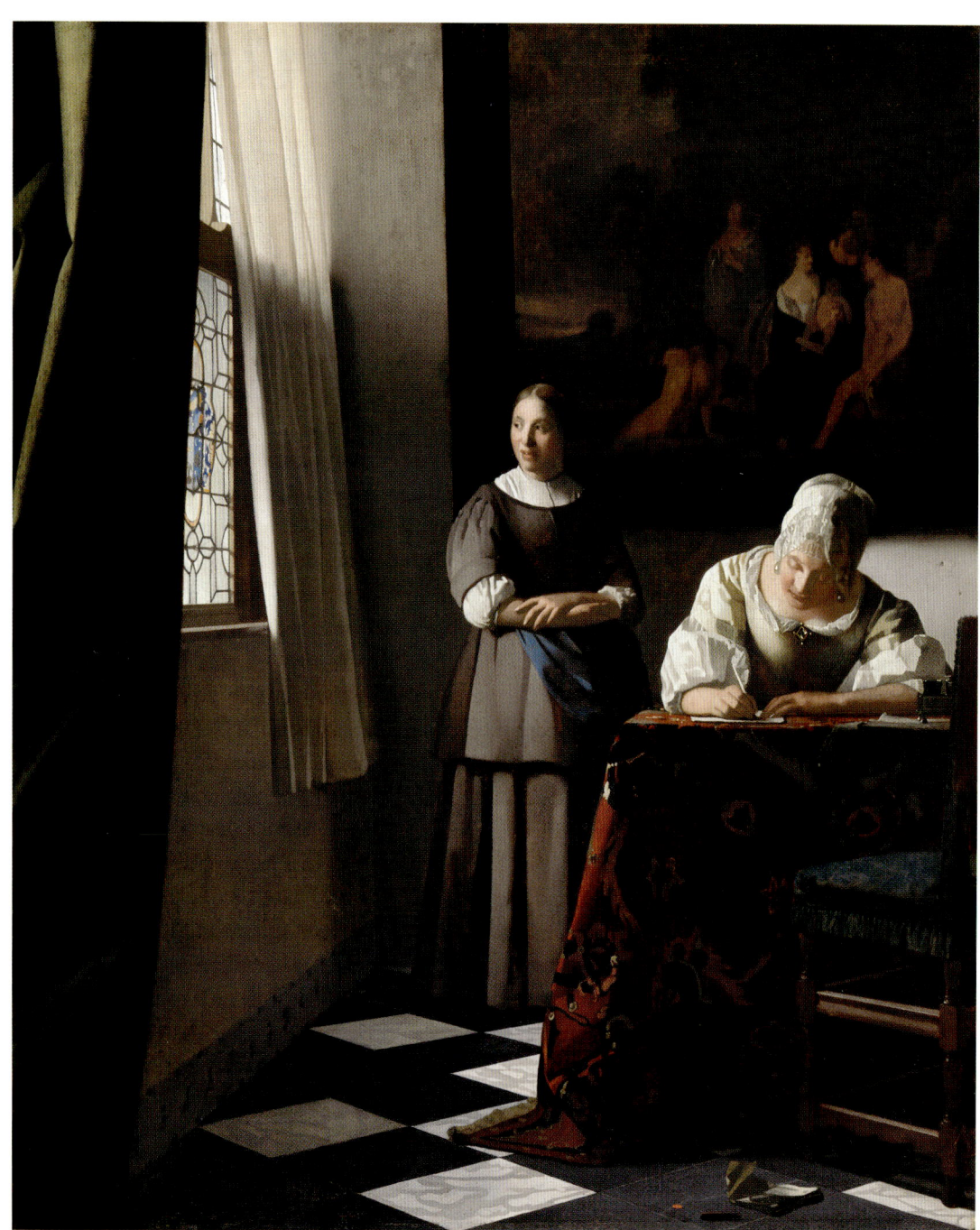

CAT. 3

Johannes Vermeer
Woman Writing a Letter with Her Maid, ca. 1670–72
Oil on canvas, 28 × 23¹³⁄₁₆ in. (71.1 × 60.5 cm)
Signed on the paper hanging over the table:
IVMeer (the first three letters in ligature)
National Gallery of Ireland, Dublin

PROVENANCE:
Catharina Bolnes (ca. 1631–1687), Vermeer's widow, Delft; transferred to Hendrick van Buyten (1632–1701), Delft, as collateral to settle a debt, 1676. Josua van Belle (1637–1710), Rotterdam; his widow, Ida Catharina van Belle-van der Meijden (1658–1729), Rotterdam; her sale, Rotterdam, September 6, 1730, no. 92, fl. 155. Franco van Bleyswijck (d. 1734), Delft; his niece, Maria Catharina van der Burch (1707–1761), and Baron Hendrik van Slingelandt (1702–1759), The Hague; either to their daughter Baroness Agatha van Slingelandt (1732–1775), The Hague, or their daughter Baroness Maria Elisabeth van Slingelandt (1734–1775), The Hague; possibly to their brother, Baron Barthout van Slingelandt (1731–1798), Dordrecht, or Agatha's widower, Willem Bentinck (1721–1784), The Hague; Viktor von Miller zu Aichholz (1845–1910), Vienna; by whom sold to dealer Charles Sedelmeyer, Paris, 1881; from whom purchased, fr. 60,000, by Eugène Secrétan (1836–1899), Paris, 1881; his sale, Paris (Boussod et al.), July 1, 1889, no. 140, fr. 62,000 to dealer Boussod and Valadon. Collection Marinoni, Paris. Dealer F. Kleinberger, Paris. Alfred Beit (1853–1906), London; his brother, Sir Otto Beit, 1st Baronet (1865–1930), London; his son, Sir Alfred Beit, 2nd Baronet (1903–1994), London and Russborough (near Dublin), 1930–1987 (stolen in 1974 and 1986, recovered in 1993); by whom presented to the National Gallery of Ireland, Dublin, 1987.

SELECTED LITERATURE:
Blankert 1978, no. 27 (ca. 1671); Nash 1991, 84–87; Wheelock 1995, 156–62; Washington and The Hague 1995–96, no. 19 (ca. 1670); Liedtke 2000, 254–56; Vergara 1998; Dublin and Greenwich 2003–4, no. 39; Vergara 2003; Liedtke 2008, no. 31 (ca. 1670–71); Franits 2015, 241–44 (ca. 1670–71); Paris, Dublin, and Washington 2017–18, no. 1.6 (ca. 1670–71); Georgievska-Shine 2022, 102–4; Wieseman 2023; Amsterdam 2023, no. 35 (ca. 1670–72).

FOR THIS PAINTING, Vermeer dispenses with the anticipatory sensation of being handed a letter and focuses instead on the activity of writing itself. The painting harkens back to one of the earliest treatments of the love-letter theme by Gerard ter Borch in his *Woman Writing a Letter* from around 1655 (see fig. 3). The role of the maid as one who stands by is unique in Vermeer's oeuvre. With an understated narrative touch, the maid's presence marks time. Her arms are patiently folded and her gaze directed out the window. But this activity of waiting, however forbearing, is precisely what lends the image a subtle sense of urgency or haste. Notable, too, is that she gives her mistress enough space to form her thoughts freely. Vermeer in this case completely reverses the motif of the onlooker peering over the shoulder of the letter writer that one finds, for example, in Ter Borch's *Curiosity* (see fig. 37). As with Ter Borch's painting, however, we have the sense of being the onlooker of a staged scene. To emphasize this, Vermeer added a curtain that has been drawn aside, so that we are presented with a scene rather than feeling like an imaginary viewer within it, as with *Mistress and Maid* (cat. 1), or a direct participant from a distance, per the staging of the *Love Letter* (cat. 2).

The most curious motif in the painting is the cluster of objects on the floor in front of the table: some folded paper with a crumpled cover, a circular red wax seal, and a stick of sealing wax.[163] The presence of the stick of wax suggests that she was in the process of sealing a letter she had just written, then changed her mind and decided to write a different one. It is not entirely clear, however, that the paper on the floor is in fact a letter since it appears to have a cover of a different color from the material it enfolds. It could be a pamphlet of some sort, but given the letter-writing context it seems more likely to be a light-brown wrapping used to protect a handwritten letter.[164] In any case, the casual discarding of these objects adds a note of agitation to the image. They serve, on a more basic level, to remove any doubts that the letter-writing activity is an affair of the heart, much as the ace-of-hearts playing card does in Ter Borch's *Officer Writing a Letter with a Trumpeter* (see fig. 25). It is telling that both artists placed these objects on the floor in the foreground.

The other element of the image that leads to speculation is the painting in the background. Its subject is the Finding of Moses (Exodus 2:1–10), in which the pharaoh's daughter, called Thermuthis by Flavius Josephus and other sources, discovers the infant Moses floating in a basket while she bathes with her handmaidens. Thermuthis rescues and raises the child, saving him from her father's decree that all Hebrew infants be killed.[165] While the painting does not appear to have survived, and we can only speculate as to who painted it, the question remains whether Vermeer intended a direct relationship with the subject of his painting.[166] One idea put forward is that the *juffrouw* writing the letter wishes protection for her recipient, much as Moses was cared for through both divine and human intervention in being found.[167] Another idea is that Vermeer meant to equate the positive virtues of the young woman with those of the pharaoh's daughter.[168] A simpler, and perhaps more directly applicable, parallel can be found in the notion of confidentiality between Thermuthis and her handmaidens: it would have been

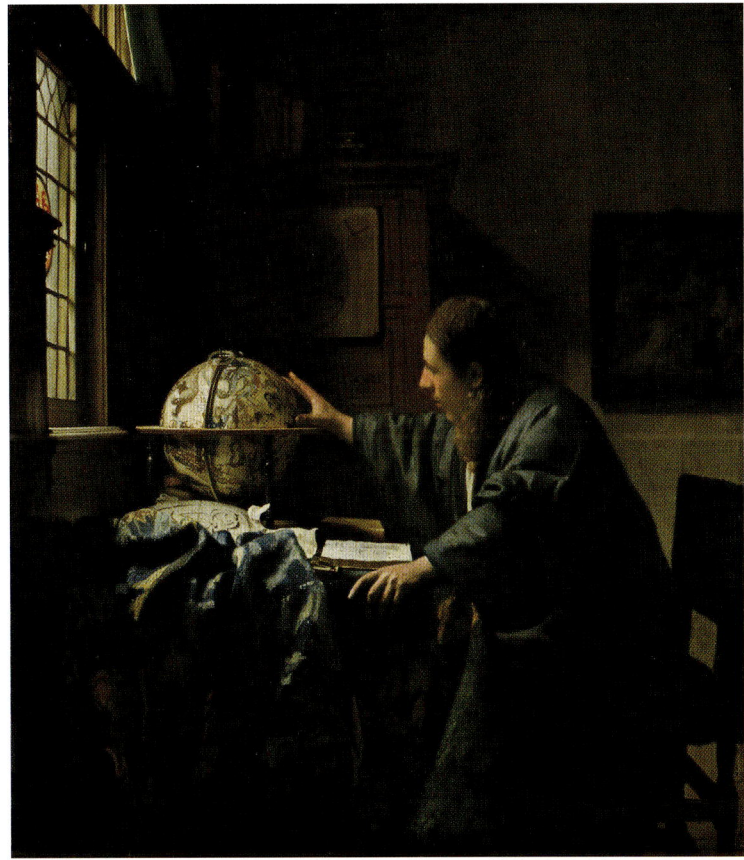

necessary for Thermuthis's attendants to keep her secrets in order for her rescue of Moses to escape the notice of her father.[169] A complicating factor in any interpretation of the painting is the fact that Vermeer had also used it in the background of a completely different type of work, his *Astronomer* from 1668 (fig. 48), in which he reduced its scale. Whatever meaning, if any, he intended in his use of the Finding of Moses in the background of these two works remains difficult to determine.

Recent technical analysis has revealed that this canvas was cut from the same bolt as three other paintings by Vermeer: *Young Woman with a Lute* (see fig. 46), *Woman with a Pearl Necklace* (Gemäldegalerie, Staatliche Museen zu Berlin), and *Woman Holding a Balance* (National Gallery of Art, Washington).[170] None of these paintings bears a date, but by general agreement they are thought to be from the early 1660s. *Woman Writing a Letter with Her Maid*, on the other hand, has long been assumed to date to around 1670 or just after. There is evidence that this painting was primed at a different moment than the other three, but the discrepancy in date is so significant that one wonders if it might have been executed earlier.[171] It nevertheless stands in our currently accepted chronology of the artist's works as the last of his letter-themed paintings.[172]

NOTES

1   For the development of the love-letter theme in Dutch painting, see, especially, Dublin and Greenwich 2003–4. For Vermeer's paintings of the subject, in particular, see Nevitt 2001, 103–8; Vergara 2003; and Wieseman 2023. For important studies of individual paintings, see Vergara 1998; Iacono 2018; and Dresden 2021. For letters and reading as themes in Dutch art generally, see Frankfurt 1993–94.

2   For a major overview of Dutch genre painting in these years, see Franits 2004, 95–14.

3   For an overview of known prices paid, see Bakker 2017–18.

4   Paris, Dublin, and Washington 2017–18; Ho 2017.

5   For Vermeer's biography, the most thorough work remains Montias 1989; more recently, see, especially, Roelofs 2023.

6   Philadelphia, Berlin, and London 1984, no. 46; Frankfurt 1993–94, no. 35; Sutton 2003, 15–17; Dublin and Greenwich 2003–4, no. 2, 82–84.

7   De Jongh 1967, 52.

8   For Vermeer's uses of paintings in the backgrounds of his works, see Arasse 1994, 22–39; and Weber 1998.

9   Gudlaugsson 1959–60, 1: 101–3, 2: no. 114; Sutton 2003, 17–21; Dublin and Greenwich 2003–4, no. 5, 90–92; Suchtelen et al. 2016, no. 3, 56–61.

10 My thanks to Naomi Bisping, academic researcher at the Rijksmuseum, for kindly providing information about this inkstand and its possible functions.

11 For Gesina ter Borch, see, especially, Kettering 1988 and Eaker 2024.

12 Washington and Detroit 2004, no. 17, 84–86; Liedtke 2007, no. 13, 63–66.

13 For the document, see Montias 1989, 102–3; for the artistic relationship, see Waiboer 2010–11.

14 Montias 1989, 103–5; Liedtke 2008, 20–21.

15 On this subject, see, most recently, Seifert 2023.

16 For this painting, see especially Dresden 2021.

17 Regarding this bodice and a surviving example, see Neidhardt 2021–22, 162–66.

18 Schölzel 2021–22.

19 Weber 2021–22.

20 Washington and The Hague 1995–96, no. 9, 134–39; Georgievska-Shine 2022, 98–103.

21 For a link between the jewelry and the love letter, see Weber (2022, 135–37), discussing both as referents to vanity in the works of Adriaen Poiters.

22 Liedtke 2008, 114.

23 Kuijpers 1997.

24 Frankfurt 1993–94, no. 49, 232–33.

25 London and Hartford 1998–99, no. 39, 176–77; Dublin and Greenwich 2003–4, no. 37, 178–79; Delft 2019, no. 23, 186–87.

26 Couchman and Crab 2005; Daybell and Gordon 2016; Van Elk 2017.

27 For women in the Republic of Letters, see Pal 2012; Van Elk 2017; and Capern 2020.

28 Smits-Veld 1998.

29 Larsen 2016.

30 For Huygens's correspondence with women, see Huysman and Leerintveld 2014.

31 Houbraken 1718–21, 1: 312: *Andere hebben weder haar brein gescherpt op taalgeleertheid, of andere prysselyke wetenschappen. Vele Vrouwen hebben de eedle zwaneschagt gevoert, en de wysheid boven alle vergankelyke schatten bemind en uitgekozen.*

32 Washington and The Hague 1995–96, no. 13, 156–59; Dublin and Greenwich 2003–4, no. 38, 181–84; Liedtke 2008, no. 20, 122–25.

33 Dublin and Greenwich 2003–4, no. 20, 133–35; Waiboer 2023.

34 For some attempt at identifying figures in Vermeer's paintings with family members, see Binstock 2009.

35 For the painting in the background, see Weber 2022, 137n.53.

36 For images of female servants in Dutch and Flemish art, see, especially, Wolfthal 2019; Wolfthal 2013; and Franits 1993, 100–110.

37 Dekker 2013, 141–43.

38 Carlson 2006, 227.

39 Watteeuw 2015, 55–56.

40 For summaries of Rembrandt's relationships with his servants, see Wolfthal 2019, 238–39; and Dudok van Heel 2001, 24–25, with further references.

41 Wolfthal 2019, 239–41. The story of Maria van Oosterwijck training her maid comes down to us via Houbraken 1718–21, 2: 214–17; see also Dabbs 2009, 160–66.

42   For Vermeer and Dou, see Ducos 2017–18 and New York 2009.

43   Hoet and Terwestern 1752–70, 1: no. 8, 34: *Een dronke slapende Meyd aen een Tafel.*

44   The Hague and London 2019–20, no. 9, 84–87.

45   Sutton 1980, no. 52, 92.

46   Wolfthal 2019, 232–33.

47   Sarnowiec 2001, 200–201; Carlson 2006, 230.

48   Carlson 2006, 230. Servants were forbidden to wear silk, velvet, lace, silver, gold, gemstones, etc., because, as the ordinance put it, "little or no distinction between the clothing of ladies and of *dienstboden* (servants) can be seen."

49   Franits 1989.

50   Waiboer 2012, no. A-126, 136–37; Paris, Dublin, and Washington 2017–18, no. 8.4, 160. For maids with similar dress in Metsu's paintings, see Waiboer 2012, nos. A–39, A–118, and A–119.

51   Schama 1980. This study was subsequently expanded into a chapter in Schama 1987, 375–480. For an important recent study, see Peacock 2020.

52   For this series, see, especially, Peacock 1993–94.

53   Delft 2019, no. 16, 166–67.

54   De Vries 1682. On this publication, see Schama 1980, 10–11; Schama 1987, 456–58; Baggerman 1993, 186–88; Carlson 1993, 246–50; and Sarnowiec 2001. Nevitt (2001, 105) drew a connection between Vermeer's letter theme and the *Seven Duyvelen.*

55   For the German book, see Sarnowiec 2001, 220n.2.

56   Anon. 1682. See Baggerman (1993, 188–92), who also suggests that the author might be Catholic. For a comparison of the illustrations between the two versions, see Sarnowiec 2001.

57   De Vries 1682, 237–63.

58   For a discussion of this illustration, see Sarnowiec 2001, 207–9.

59   Sarnowiec 2001, 200–201; Carlson 2006, 230.

60   Carlson 2006, 229–30.

61   Wolfthal 2019, 238–39.

62   Anon. 1697.

63   For discussions of the *Seve Engelen*, see Baggerman 1993, 192–94; and Carlson 1994, 90.

64   Anon. 1697, 73–74.

65   Anon. 1697, 39–40.

66   Opinions are divided on this issue. For the suggestion that the author might be a woman, see Baggerman 1993, 193n.1; and that it might be a man, Carlson 1994, 90n.15. Perhaps telling is that the publisher is the Weduwe (Widow) Van Damme.

67   For the translation, see Montias 1989, 160. For the document, dated July 3, 1666, see Montias 1989, 324, doc. no. 305.

68   Montias 1989, 160.

69   For the story of Maria Gerrits, see Montias 1989, 164–69. Montias chose to call her Mary to distinguish her more easily from Maria Thins, but her name appears with slight variations in documents: Maria Gerards de Veer in doc. no. 302, May 23, 1666, but also as Marij Gerrits van Waelwijck (today spelled Waalrijk, a town to the west of Den Bosch) in doc. no. 306, July 18, 1666.

70   Montias 1989, 164.

71   Montias 1989, 196 and 327, doc. no. 317, May 2, 1668.

72   Montias 1989, 317, doc. no. 290, May 14, 1662.

73   Montias 1989, 344–45, doc. no. 367, April 24 and 30, 1676 (spelled Tanneken, first name only, which is probably indicative of familiarity).

74   Montias 1989, 161. This later dating of *The Milkmaid* to 1660–61 can be found, for example, in Blankert 1978, 157n.7.

75   Gudlaugsson 1959–60, no. 144; Blankert 1995–96, 39; Dublin and Greenwich 2003–4, no. 9, 101–4; Washington and Detroit 2004, no. 33, 132–34.

76   Gudlaugsson 1959–60, no. 143; Philadelphia, Berlin, and London 1984, no. 10; Frankfurt 1993–94, no. 11; Kettering 2000, 110–15; Dublin and Greenwich 2003–4, no. 8, 99–102; Washington and Detroit 2004, no. 32, 129–31.

77   They were first identified as pendants by Peter Sutton; see Dublin and Greenwich 2003–4, 104.

78   Dublin and Greenwich 2003–4, nos. 16 and 17, 124–27; Waiboer 2012, 78–80.

79   Dublin and Greenwich 2003–4, nos. 18 and 19, 128–33; Dublin, Amsterdam, and Washington 2010, 38–42; Waiboer 2012, 122–25.

80   For curtains as a topos in Dutch art, see Fucci 2015 and Fucci 2021–22.

81   For restraint and other aspects of the courting *vryster* generally, see Franits 1993, 33–61.

82   Sneller and Thijs 1993; Sutton 2003, 39–40.

83   Transcribed and translated in Sutton 2003, 39–40 (the translation adapted here): *Neem eens, ick kreegh een jonghman life, / Sal ick niet soetjens, met een brief, / Hem mogen klagen mijnen noot? / 't Papier en kent geen eerbaer root, / Den pen en inckt doen menighwerf / Dat mont en tonge iet en derf.*

84   Sutton 2003.

85   One of the most popular was Jean Puget de la Serre's *La Secrétaire à la mode* (1630), translated into

Dutch as the *Fatsoenlicke zend-brief-schryver* (1651) but also issued in the original French in Amsterdam at least nineteen times between 1643 and 1664. See Sutton 2003, 33, with further references.

86   This text comes directly from a contemporary English translation; De la Serre 1668, 71.

87   Moulton 2010, 231.

88   De la Serre 1668, 71.

89   Moulton 2010, 232.

90   See, for example, the letter from the Frenchwoman Anne-Marie Martinozzi (1637–1672) to her husband: "My dear husband, I have never loved you so much. I feel a tenderness in the bottom of my heart for you, greater it seems to me than I have ever felt." Hillman 2015, 74; cited in Georgievska-Shine 2022, 100.

91   For a study of the Dutch vernacular tradition of the *Heroides*, see Marion 2005.

92   For a comprehensive list of translations or adaptations of the *Heroides* into Dutch, see Van Marion 2005, 361–81.

93   Ibid., 69–71.

94   Ibid., 82–89.

95   Ovid/Isbell 1990, 94.

96   For the importance of Ovid and the *Ars Amatoria* for Dutch art, see Van Boheemen 1989; and for its relation to Vermeer, see Vergara 2003, 55, noting the importance of the vernacular translations.

97   Ovid/Mozley 1979, 93.

98   Ibid., 165.

99   Ibid., 173.

100 Ovid/Visscher 1625.

101 Ovid/Laurier 1564.

102 Ovid/Bouman 1660.

103 Westerbaen 1665. In relation to Vermeer's letter-themed paintings, the connection with Westerbaen's *Avond-School* has been raised by H. Rodney Nevitt; see Nevitt 2001, 106. See also Vergara 2003, 52, noting (in relation to Vermeer's *Girl Reading a Letter at an Open Window* in Dresden) Westerbaen's advice in the *Avond-School* to send fruit to your lover.

104 Van Heemskerk 1626.

105 Westerbaen 1665, 3: *Dit was die soeten Baes, die eertyds heeft beschreven / Hoe dat men op zyn Rooms de meysjes vryen most: / Wel, dacht ick, of ick dat eens op zyn Haegs begost? / En heb dat Roomse Kleed ontarrent en versneden, / Gelanght, gekort, gelast, gepast nae onse leden, / En uyt de Lessen van dien geestigen Pöeet / Een nieuwe Minne-kunst voor onse Jeugd gesmeedt.* Translation my own.

106 Westerbaen 1665, 69–70: *Al werd ghy naeu bewae-ckt: ghy vind gelegentheyd / Om aen u vryer yet t' onbieden door u meyd: / Ghy vindt gelegentheyd om heen en weer te schrijven: / Uw briefjes kunnen gaen en 't kan verhoolen blijven. / Geen stad werdt oyt so dicht belegert en bewaeckt / Daer niet somtijds een boo of briefjen in geraeckt. / Daer zijn veel middelen van schrijven en bestellen: / Den boesem van uw meyd sal van geen briefje swellen. / Men bergse daer, of in haer koussens, in haer schoen, / Indien men in haer zack huys-zoecking quam te doen.* Translation my own. See also Nevitt 2001, 106, for a translation of the first four lines.

107 For Westerbaen and his publications, see Koppenol 2001. Westerbaen had also translated a number of letters from the *Heroides* into Dutch, published in a collection of verses; see Westerbaen 1657.

108 For a letter from Westerbaen to Huygens (introduced and transcribed by Eric Jorink), see Huysman and Leerintveld 2022, 204–9.

109 Haarlem and London 2008, 18–19, 116–17; Weber 1987.

110 Cited in Verdier 1983, 45.

111 Anon. 1669.

112 Anon. 1678, 7.

113 For the reception history of the *Lettres Portugaises*, see O'Leary 2024, 369–70; Kauffman 1988, 95–96; and Verdier 1983, 47.

114 The Amsterdam edition was published by Isaac van Dyck, with the slightly modified title *Lettres d'une religieuse portugaise*, no doubt to sensationalize the fact that the letter writer was a nun.

115 Verdier 1983, 48.

116 Ibid., 46–49; Kauffman 1988, 92–94. Plausible candidates have been put forward for both the nun, Marianna Alcoforado (1640–1723), a nun in Beja who came from a wealthy family, and the officer, Noël Bouton, the marquis de Chamilly (1636–1715).

117 For the relationship between the real and the fictional in the *Lettres Portugaises* and the epistolary culture that followed, see Bray 2024.

118 Green 2021, 22. For the painting by De Hooch, see Delft 2019, no. 10, 148–49.

119 Green 2021, 20–22.

120 Ibid., 21.

121 The *Mistress and Maid* in The Frick Collection was already described in an auction catalogue from 1738 as a woman being brought a letter *in haar binnenkamer* (in her inner room); see Grijzenhout 2010, 68.

122 Kettering 1993. For the Petrarchan model in relation to Vermeer's works, see Zell 2011.

123 Montias 1989, 98–108. As Montias notes, Maria Thins's objection could have been more socially based since her family was much wealthier than Vermeer's.

124 Koppenol 2001, 112–13.

125 The comprehensive study of the Ter Borch albums is Kettering 1988.

126 Kettering 1988, 2: 629, 692: fol. 27 recto of the Family Scrapbook, dated 1661.

127 For the painting in Helsinki, see Dublin and Greenwich 2003–4, no. 10, 105–7; and Washington and Detroit 2004, no. 41, 154–57. In one of her collected song verses, Gesina illustrates it with men drinking away their love sorrows. See Amsterdam, Rijksprentenkabinet, Poetry Album (inv. no. BI–1890-1952), fol. 83; Kettering 1988, 2: 461; Gudlaugsson 1959–60, 2: 139; cited by Peter Sutton in Dublin and Greenwich 2003–4, 106.

128 Ovid/Mozley 1979, 233, given with slight modifications here.

129 For this idea, see Eaker 2024.

130 The essential study that convincingly revealed these patrons is Montias 1987; but see also Montias 1989, 246–57.

131 For recently discovered evidence that argues even more fully for Maria de Knuijt's primary role in Vermeer's patronage, see Noorman and Bakker forthcoming.

132 Hoet and Terwestern 1752–70, 1: 34. The original auction catalogue does not survive, but it was transcribed by Gerard Hoet, who published it along with the prices the paintings achieved at auction.

133 See Grijzenhout 2010, in which the Dissius painting is convincingly argued to be the *Mistress and Maid* in The Frick Collection on the basis of a household inventory for Jacob Oortman (1661–1738) in which it appears that he had purchased at least two other paintings from the 1696 Dissius sale.

134 For Van Buyten, see Montias 1989, 258–61. This amount of bread, according to Montias's calculation, would have fed Vermeer's large family for about three years, indicating that the debt began to build up around the time of the great financial collapse in 1672 (the *rampjaar*, or disaster year). For the document transferring the paintings, see Bredius 1885, 219–20; Blankert 1978, 149–50, doc. no. 37; and Montias 1989, 338, doc. no. 361.

135 Montias 1989, 180. Bathazar de Monconys recorded in his journal visiting a baker in Delft, where he had been sent to see a painting by Vermeer after being told by the artist that he had no paintings in his own house to show him. The painting is simply described as depicting a single figure. For Van Buyten's collection, as listed in his 1701 postmortem inventory, which includes his three Vermeer paintings, see Montias 1989, 364–65, doc. no. 442.

136 *d'eene vertonende twee personagien waeroff d'een een brieff sit te schrijven, ende d'ander mede een personagie spelende op een cyter.* Transcription taken from Blankert 1978, 149–50, doc. no. 37.

137 For the darkening of the pigment, see Iacono 2018, 39–40.

138 For Vermeer's use of curtains generally, see Fucci 2021–22.

139 "Een schrijvent juffertje in haar binnenkamer die een brief ontfangt," auctioned in the Keizerkroon, Amsterdam, October 15–16, 1738. On this, see Grijzenhout 2010, 68.

140 Iacono 2018, 40–45.

141 Vandivere et al. 2019.

142 For the pearls in Vermeer's works, see Roelofs 2023, 212, and Iacono 2018, 26–27.

143 Roelofs 2023, 62. Also, see Amsterdam 2023, 292, on the model for the mantle, which was likely the one found in the estate inventory of Catharina Bolnes in 1676, listed as "a yellow satin mantle with white fur trim" (Een geele zatijne mantel met witte bonte kanten).

144 See Chong 2013, 9 (paragraph 27); and Wieseman 2023, 236–37.

145 For the dating of these two paintings, see, most recently, Amsterdam 2023, nos. 21 and 22, putting them both ca. 1664–67. For an opposing view, see Wadum (1998, 213–14), linking the painting to early works like *A Maid Asleep*, and speculating that *Mistress and Maid* could have come from earlier in his career.

146 Wheelock (1995, 142) was the first to argue against the unfinished nature of the painting, a view that has met general acceptance. Given the painting's *sfumato*, some have wondered about a connection with the ideas about painting put forward by Leonardo da Vinci, whose notebooks first appeared in print in 1652, translated into French; see Wadum 1998, 205–7; and Arasse 1994, 73–74.

147 "Een Juffrouw die door een Meyd een brief gebragt word." See Hoet and Terwestern 1752–70, 1: 34, no. 7.

148 Liedtke 2000, 242.

149　On the statement made by Sir Charles Eastlake (1793–1865), see Iacono 2018, 34, and Jowell 1998, 49. Eastlake, in trying to acquire it for the National Gallery, London, offered the owner 5,000 francs, instead of the asking price of 7,500 francs, and was declined.

150　For the differences between a cittern and a guitar, and some seventeenth-century examples, see London 2013, 73 and passim.

151　For Vermeer's musical figures and those who "invite duets," see London 2013 and Wieseman 2017.

152　As first noted by De Jongh (1967, 50), who mentions an emblem by Jan Harmensz Krul from his 1634 *Minnebeelden* (Images of Love) with the motto "Although you are far away, you are in my heart" (Al zyt ghy vert, noyt uyt het hert) and further verses comparing love to a sea. For this relation, see also Washington and The Hague 1995–96, 182; Goodman 2001, 76–78; Sutton 2003–4, 18; Franits 2015, 239–41; and Weber 2023, 189–90.

153　See Hollander 2002, 7–47, on this type of perspectival view (called a *doorkijkje* or *doorzien*), which has a long tradition in Netherlandish and Dutch art.

154　This painting has often been associated with Pieter de Hooch's *Couple with a Parrot* (Wallraf-Richartz-Museum, Cologne) since it has a similar composition. See, for example, Washington and The Hague 1995–96, 180, and Liedtke 2000, 253. Because De Hooch's painting was long thought to bear a date of 1668, it raised the issue of whether he perhaps influenced Vermeer in this case. As Peter Sutton has pointed out, however, De Hooch's painting is, in fact, undated, and likely came later. See London and Hartford 1998–99, no. 40 (ca. 1675–77), and Sutton 2003–4, 186.

155　The linen basket and sewing cushion no doubt belong to the *juffrouw*. See Franits (1993, 48), with the suggestion that they signal the young woman's preoccupation with love since she set them aside to practice her cittern.

156　Regarding the map, Landsman (2022, 88–91) notes the special challenge in this case of depicting the map at an oblique angle. For the two other works in which the map appears, see Landsman 2022, 107–8.

157　For the most complete discussion of the provenance, see Washington and The Hague 1995–96, 182–85.

158　"Een Juffrouw die door een Meyd een brief gebragt word." See Hoet and Terwesten 1752–70, 1: 34, no. 7.

159　*. . . d'eene vertonende twee personagien waeroff d'een een brieff sit te schrijven, ende d'ander mede een personagie spelende op een cyter.* See Blankert 1978, 149, doc. no. 37; and Montias 1989, 338, doc. no. 361.

160　This aspect of the provenance was clarified in Grijzenhout 2010. Also, see the entry for cat. 1 in the present publication.

161　This theory was no longer tenable once Montias (1987) established that the 1696 Dissius auction included the collection of De Knuijt and Van Ruijven. It had been surmised previously (e.g., Blankert 1978, no. 28) that *The Guitar Player* reached the Dissius sale after having been in the hands of Van Buyten.

162　It was Van Buyten himself who noted Catharina's plea in a second version of the contract: "bewogen door 't serieus versoeck ende instantelijck aenhouden van de voorsz. transportante" (moved by the serious plea and urgent persistence of the aforementioned transferor). See Blankert 1978, 338, doc. no. 37 (with the original transcription); and Montias 1989, 338, doc. no. 361. For an overview of Catharina's life and financial problems after Vermeer's death, see Montias 1989, 216–45; and related documents.

163　The wax seal and stick of sealing wax, for many years overpainted, came to light in 1974 when the painting was cleaned, for which see O'Connor 1977.

164　For the suggestion that the object is a booklet, specifically a volume of model love letters, see Blankert 1995, 39. For considerations of this cluster of objects, see Washington and The Hague 1995–96, 188 ("Letters were highly valued and not objects to be thrown aside, except, perhaps, in anger."); Vergara 1998, 240 (suggesting that Vermeer intentionally meant to encourage speculation); Liedtke 2000, 255–56; Vergara 2003, 58; Sutton 2003–4, 188; and Georgievska-Shine 2022, 103–4.

165　For Thermuthis and sources related to her, see Vergara 1998, 238.

166　See Blankert (1978, 166), and Foucart (1989) for ideas about the authorship of the painting, the most persistent of which is that it was possibly made by Peter Lely (1618–1680). For Vermeer's use of the picture-within-a-picture generally, see Weber 1998.

167　Wheelock 1995, 162.

168　This is the central thesis of Vergara 1998, which remains the most extensive iconographic study of the painting.

169 See Georgievska-Shine 2022, 103, for the idea that the maid in Vermeer's painting is likewise a keeper of secrets and "privy to the sentiments of her mistress that will be inscribed in that letter."

170 See Johnson 2017 (online), Appendix II, Match 3. Instead of thread counting, this innovative technique uses weave-density maps to match canvases cut from the same bolt. For the three matching paintings, see Amsterdam 2023, nos. 18 (ca. 1662–64), 19 (ca. 1662–64), and 20 (ca. 1662–64).

171 See Wiedema 2021–22 on the difference in priming that was reported by Ige Verslype to Michiel Franken.

172 For the most current chronology of Vermeer's paintings, see Amsterdam 2023, 6–16, the dates of which are adopted throughout the present publication. Perhaps significant is that this painting was in older scholarship assumed to have been made earlier. See, for example, De Vries 1939, no. 21, 85–86, wherein it is dated ca. 1660–62.

BIBLIOGRAPHY

Amsterdam 2023
  Pieter Roelofs and Gregor J. M. Weber et al. *Vermeer*. Exh. cat. Amsterdam (Rijksmuseum), 2023.

Anon. 1669
  Anonymous (Mariana Alcoforado or Gabriel-Joseph de Lavergne?). *Lettres Portugaises*. Paris, 1669.

Anon. 1678
  Anonymous (Mariana Alcoforado or Gabriel-Joseph de Lavergne?). *Five Love-Letters from a Nun to a Cavalier*. London, 1678.

Anon. 1682
  Anonymous (signed "Liefhebber van Dienstmaagden"). *Zeven Duivelen, Regerende en Vervoerende de Hedendaagsche Dienst-Maagden*. Amsterdam, 1682.

Anon. 1697
  J. H. B. (initials only). *De Seve Engelen Der Dienst-maagden. Zijnde een Rare en Beknopte Wederlegginge, tegen een nu-onlangs uitgegeve Boekje, genaamd De 7 Duivelen der Dienst-maagden*. Leiden, 1697.

Apeldoorn 1989
  Petra van Boheemen et al. *Kent, en versint, Eer datje mint: Vrijen en trouwen 1500–1800*. Exh. cat. Apeldoorn (Historisch Museum Marialust), 1989.

Arasse 1994
  Arasse, Daniel. *Vermeer: Faith in Painting*. Princeton, 1994.

Baggerman 1993
  Baggerman, Arianne. *Een drukkend gewicht: Leven en werk van de zeventiende-eeuwse veelschrijver Simon de Vries*. Amsterdam and Atlanta, 1993.

Bakker 2017–18
  Bakker, Piet. "Painters of and for the Elite: Relationships, Prices and Familiarity with Each Other's Works." In Paris, Dublin, and Washington 2017–18, 85–99, 268–69.

Binstock 2009
  Binstock, Benjamin. *Vermeer's Family Secrets: Genius, Discovery, and the Unknown Apprentice*. New York and London, 2009.

Blankert 1978
  Blankert, Albert. *Vermeer of Delft: Complete Edition of the Paintings*. Oxford, 1978.

Blankert 1995–96
  Blankert, Albert. "Vermeer's Modern Themes and Their Tradition." In Washington and The Hague 1995–96, 31–45.

Bray 2024
  Bray, Joe. "The Letter-Writing Manual and the Epistolary Novel." *Journal for Eighteenth-Century Studies* 47, no. 1 (2024): 15–29.

Bredius 1885
  Bredius, Abraham. "Iets over Johannes Vermeer ('De Delftsche Vermeer')." *Oud Holland* 3 (1885): 217–22.

Capern 2020
  Capern, Amanda L. "Literature and Letters." In *The Routledge History of Women in Early Modern Europe*, edited by Amanda L. Capern, 404–26. Abingdon and New York, 2020.

Carlson 1993
  Carlson, Marybeth. "Domestic Service in a Changing City Economy: Rotterdam 1680–1780." PhD diss., University of Wisconsin–Madison, 1993.

Carlson 1994
  Carlson, Marybeth. "A Trojan Horse of Worldliness? Maidservants in the Burgher Household in Rotterdam at the End of the Seventeenth Century." In *Women of the Golden Age: An International Debate on Women in Seventeenth-Century Holland, England and Italy*, edited by Els Kloek, Nicole Teeuwen, and Marijke Huisman, 87–96. Hilversum, 1994.

Carlson 2006
  Carlson, Marybeth. "'There Is No Service Here but My Service!': Municipal Attempts to Regulate Domestic Servant Behavior in Early Modern Holland." In *Power and the City in the Netherlandic World*, edited by Wayne te Brake and Wim Klooster, 225–34. Leiden and Boston, 2006.

Chong 2013
  Chong, Alan. "Sri Lankan Ivories for the Dutch and Portuguese." *Journal of Historians of Netherlandish Art* 5, no. 2 (2013): 1–14.

Couchman and Crab 2005
  Couchman, Jane, and Ann Crab, eds. *Women's Letters across Europe, 1400–1700: Form and Persuasion*. Farnham, UK, 2005.

Dabbs 2009

    Dabbs, Julia K. *Life Stories of Women Artists, 1550–1800: An Anthology.* Farnham, UK, and Burlington, 2009.

Daybell and Gordon 2016

    Daybell, James, and Andrew Gordon, eds. *Women and Epistolary Agency in Early Modern Culture, 1450–1690.* London and New York, 2016.

De Jongh 1967

    De Jongh, Eddy. *Zinne- en minnebeelden in de schilderkunst van de zeventiende eeuw.* Amsterdam, 1967.

Dekker 2013

    Dekker, Rudolf. *Family, Culture and Society in the Diary of Constantijn Huygens Jr.* Leiden, 2013.

De la Serre 1651

    De la Serre, Jean Puget. *Fatsoenlicke Zend-brief-Schryver.* Translated from the French by I. D. Amsterdam, 1651.

De la Serre 1668

    De la Serre, Jean Puget. *The Secretary in Fashion, or, An Elegant and Compendious Way of Writing all Manner of Letters.* London, 1668.

Delft 2019

    Anita Jansen et al. *Pieter de Hooch in Delft: In the Shadow of Vermeer.* Exh. cat. Delft (Museum Prinsenhof Delft), 2019.

De Vries 1682

    De Vries, Simon. *Seven Duyvelen, Regerende en Vervoerende de Hedensdaeghsche Dienst-Maegden.* Amsterdam, 1682.

De Vries 1939

    De Vries, A. B. *Jan Vermeer van Delft.* Amsterdam, 1939.

Dresden 2021–22

    Stephan Koja, Uta Neidhardt, and Arthur K. Wheelock Jr., eds. *Johannes Vermeer: On Reflection.* Exh. cat. Dresden (Staatliche Kunstsammlungen Dresden), 2021–22.

Dublin and Greenwich 2003–4

    Peter C. Sutton et al. *Love Letters: Dutch Genre Paintings in the Age of Vermeer.* Exh. cat. Dublin (National Gallery of Ireland) and Greenwich, CT (Bruce Museum of Arts and Sciences), 2003–4.

Dublin, Amsterdam, and Washington 2010–11

    Adriaan E. Waiboer et al. *Gabriel Metsu.* Exh. cat. Dublin (National Gallery of Ireland), Amsterdam (Rijksmuseum), and Washington (National Gallery of Art), 2010–11.

Ducos 2017–18

    Ducos, Blaise. "Maids and Morals." In Paris, Dublin, and Washington 2017–18, 204–7.

Dudok van Heel 2001

    Dudok van Heel, S. A. C. "Rembrandt: His Life, His Wife, the Nursemaid and the Servant." In Edinburgh and London 2001, 19–27.

Eaker 2024

    Eaker, Adam. *Gesina ter Borch.* London, 2024.

Edinburgh and London 2001

    Julia Lloyd Williams et al. *Rembrandt's Women.* Exh. cat. Edinburgh (National Gallery of Scotland) and London (Royal Academy of Arts), 2001.

Foucart 1989

    Foucart, Jacques. "Peter Lely, Dutch History Painter." *Hoogsteder-Naumann Mercury* 8 (1989): 17–26.

Franits 1989

    Franits, Wayne E. "The Depiction of Servants in Some Paintings by Pieter de Hooch." *Zeitschrift für Kunstgeschichte* 52, no. 4 (1989): 559–66.

Franits 1993

    Franits, Wayne E. *Paragons of Virtue: Women and Domesticity in Seventeenth-Century Dutch Art.* Cambridge, UK, 1993.

Franits 2001

    Franits, Wayne E., ed. *The Cambridge Companion to Vermeer.* Cambridge, UK, 2001.

Franits 2004

    Franits, Wayne E. *Dutch Seventeenth-Century Genre Painting: Its Stylistic and Thematic Evolution.* New Haven, 2004.

Franits 2015

    Franits, Wayne E. *Vermeer.* London, 2015.

Frankfurt 1993–94

    Sabine Schulze et al. *Leselust: Niederländische Malerei von Rembrandt bis Vermeer.* Exh. cat. Frankfurt (Schirn Kunsthalle), 1993–94.

Fucci 2015

    Fucci, Robert. "Parrhasius and the Art of Display: The Illusionistic Curtain in Seventeenth-Century Dutch Painting." *Nederlands Kunsthistorisch Jaarboek* 65 (2015): 144–75.

Fucci 2021–22

    Fucci, Robert. "Curtains and Perspectives: Vermeer's Optical Realism." In Dresden 2021–22, 97–121.

Gaskell and Jonker 1998

    Gaskell, Ivan, and Michiel Jonker, eds. *Vermeer Studies.* Washington, 1998.

Georgievska-Shine 2022

    Georgievska-Shine, Aneta. *Vermeer and the Art of Love.* London, 2022.

Goodman 2001

Goodman, Elise. "The Landscape on the Wall in Vermeer." In Franits 2001, 73–88.

Green 2021

Green, Michaël. "Spaces of Privacy in Early Modern Dutch Egodocuments." *The Low Countries Journal for Social and Economic History* 18, no. 3 (2021): 17–40.

Grijzenhout 2010

Grijzenhout, Frans. "Een schrijfstertje van Vermeer: Jacob Oortman en de Dissius-veiling van 1696." *Oud Holland* 123, no. 1 (2010): 65–75.

Gudlaugsson 1959–60

Gudlaugsson, S. J. *Gerard ter Borch.* 2 vols. The Hague, 1959–60.

Haarlem and London 2008

Pieter Biesboer et al. *Salomon, Jan, Joseph en Dirck de Bray: Vier schilders in één gezin.* Exh. cat. Haarlem (Frans Hals Museum) and London (Dulwich Picture Gallery), 2008.

The Hague and London 2019–20

Aariane van Suchtelen et al. *Nicolaes Maes.* Exh. cat. The Hague (Mauritshuis) and London (National Gallery of Art), 2019–20.

Hillman 2015

Hillman, Jennifer. "'Always toward Absent Lovers, Love's Tide Stronger Flows': Spiritual Lovesickness in the Letters of Anne-Marie Martinozzi." *Historical Reflections / Réflexions Historiques* 41, no. 2 (2015): 70–87.

Ho 2017

Ho, Angela K. *Creating Distinctions in Dutch Genre Painting: Repetition and Invention.* Amsterdam, 2017.

Hoet and Terwestern 1752–70

Hoet, Gerard, and Pieter Terwestern. *Catalogus of naamlijst van schilderyen, met derselver pryzen . . .* 3 vols. The Hague, 1752–70.

Hollander 2000

Hollander, Martha. "Public and Private Life in the Art of Pieter de Hooch." *Nederlands Kunsthistorisch Jaarboek* 51 (2000): 272–93.

Hollander 2002

Hollander, Martha. *An Entrance for the Eyes: Space and Meaning in Seventeenth-Century Dutch Art.* Berkeley, 2002.

Houbraken 1718–21

Houbraken, Arnold. *De groote schouburgh der Nederlantsche konstschilders en schilderessen.* 3 vols. The Hague, 1718–21. Reprint of the 1753 edition, Amsterdam, 1976.

Huysman and Leerintveld 2014

Huysman, Ineke, and Ad Leerintveld. "New Perspectives of the Digitized Correspondence of Constantijn Huygens (1596–1687)." *Dutch Crossing* 38, no. 3 (2014): 244–58.

Huysman and Leerintveld 2022

Huysman, Ineke, and Ad Leerintveld, eds. *Constantijn Huygens: Een leven in brieven.* Soest, 2022.

Iacono 2018

Iacono, Margaret. "Vermeer's Mistress and Maid." In *Vermeer's Mistress and Maid*, by Margaret Iacono and James Ivory, 17–57. New York, 2018.

Johnson 2017

Johnson, C. R., Jr., ed. *Counting Vermeer: Using Weave Maps to Study Vermeer's Canvases.* RKD Studies, 2017. https://countingvermeer.rkdstudies.nl.

Jowell 1998

Jowell, Frances Suzman. "Vermeer and Thoré-Bürger: Recoveries of Reputation." In Gaskell and Jonker 1998, 35–57.

Kauffman 1988

Kauffman, Linda. *Discourses of Desire: Gender, Genre, and Epistolary Fictions.* Ithaca, NY, 1988.

Kettering 1988

Kettering, Alison McNeil. *Drawings from the Ter Borch Studio Estate in the Rijksmuseum.* The Hague, 1988.

Kettering 1993

Kettering, Alison McNeil. "Ter Borch's Ladies in Satin." *Art History* 16, no. 1 (1993): 95–124.

Koppenol 2001

Koppenol, Johan, ed. *Jacob Westerbaen: Gedichten.* Amsterdam, 2001.

Kuijpers 1997

Kuijpers, Erika. "Lezen en schrijven: Een onderzoek naar het alfabetiseringsniveau in zeventiende-eeuws Amsterdam." *Tijdschrift voor sociale geschiedenis* 23, no. 4 (1997): 490–522.

Landsman 2022

Landsman, Rozemarijn. *Vermeer's Maps.* New York, 2022.

Larsen 2016

Larsen, Anne R. *Anna Maria van Schurman, "The Star of Utrecht": The Educational Vision and Reception of a Savante.* London, 2016.

Liedtke 2000

Liedtke, Walter. *A View of Delft: Vermeer and His Contemporaries.* Zwolle, 2000.

Liedtke 2007

Liedtke, Walter. *Dutch Paintings in the Metropolitan Museum of Art.* 2 vols. New York, 2007.

Liedtke 2008
Liedtke, Walter. *Vermeer: The Complete Paintings*. New York, 2008.

London 2013
Marjorie E. Wieseman. *Vermeer and Music: The Art of Love and Leisure*. Exh. cat. London (National Gallery), 2013.

London and Hartford 1998–99
Peter C. Sutton. *Pieter de Hooch, 1629–1684*. Exh. cat. London (Dulwich Picture Gallery) and Hartford (Wadsworth Atheneum), 1998–99.

Montias 1987
Montias, John Michael. "Vermeer's Clients and Patrons." *Art Bulletin* 69, no. 1 (1987): 242–62.

Montias 1989
Montias, John Michael. *Vermeer and His Milieu: A Web of Social History*. Princeton, 1989.

Moulton 2010
Moulton, Ian Frederick. "Modeling Female Sexuality in Early Modern Letter Books." *Early Modern Women* 5 (2010): 229–34.

Nash 1991
Nash, John. *Vermeer*. London, 1991.

Neidhardt 2021–22
Neidhardt, Uta. "Interplay of Art and Life: Vermeer's *Girl Reading a Letter at an Open Window* in a New Guise." In Dresden 2021–22, 159–91.

Nevitt 2001
Nevitt, H. Rodney, Jr. "Vermeer and the Question of Love." In *The Cambridge Companion to Vermeer*, edited by Wayne E. Franits, 89–110. Cambridge, UK, and New York, 2001.

Nevitt 2003
Nevitt, H. Rodney, Jr. *Art and the Culture of Love in Seventeenth-Century Holland*. Cambridge, UK, 2003.

New York 2009
Walter Liedtke. *The Milkmaid by Johannes Vermeer*. Exh. cat. New York (Metropolitan Museum of Art), 2009.

Noorman and Bakker forthcoming
Noorman, Judith, and Piet Bakker. "Women's Vermeers: Maria de Knuijt and New Archival Documentation on Vermeer's Clients." Proceedings from symposium in connection with Amsterdam 2023. Forthcoming.

O'Connor 1977
O'Connor, Andrew. "A Note on the Biet Vermeer." *Burlington Magazine* 119, no. 889 (1977): 272, 274–75.

O'Leary 2024
O'Leary, Jessica. "The *Lettres Portugaises*: Scripting and Selling Female Desire." *Gender & History* 36, no. 2 (2024): 369–85.

Ovid/Bouman 1660
Ovid. *De Arte Amandi, ofte De Konste der Minnen*. Printed by Jan Bouman. Amsterdam, 1660.

Ovid/Isbell 1990
Ovid. *Heroides*. Translated by Harold Isbell. London, 1990.

Ovid/Laurier 1564
Ovid. *Die Conste der Minnen*. Translated by Marius Laurier. Antwerp, 1564.

Ovid/Mozley 1979
Ovid. *The Art of Love and Other Poems*. Translated by J. H. Mozley. Cambridge, MA, and London, 1979.

Ovid/Visscher 1625
Ovid. *De Arte Amandi, or The Art of Love*. Printed by Nicolas Jansz Visscher. Amsterdam, 1625.

Paris, Dublin, and Washington 2017–18
Adriaan E. Waiboer et al. *Vermeer and the Masters of Genre Painting: Inspiration and Rivalry*. Exh. cat. Paris (Musée du Louvre), Dublin (National Gallery of Ireland), and Washington (National Gallery of Art), 2017–18.

Pal 2012
Pal, Carol. *Republic of Women: Rethinking the Republic of Letters in the Seventeenth Century*. Cambridge, UK, 2012.

Peacock 1993–94
Peacock, Martha Moffitt. "Geertruydt Roghman and the Female Perspective in 17th-Century Dutch Genre Imagery." *Woman's Art Journal* 14, no. 2 (1993–94): 3–10.

Peacock 2020
Peacock, Martha Moffitt. *Heroines, Harpies, and Housewives: Imaging Women of Consequence in the Dutch Golden Age*. Leiden and Boston, 2020.

Philadelphia, Berlin, and London 1984
Peter Sutton et al. *Masters of Seventeenth-Century Dutch Genre Painting*. Exh. cat. Philadelphia (Philadelphia Museum of Art), Berlin (Gemäldegalerie), and London (Royal Academy of Arts), 1984.

Roelofs 2023
Roelofs, Pieter. "Johannes Vermeer (Delft 1632–1675): Modestly Masterful." In Amsterdam 2023, 26–40.

Sarnowiec 2001
    Sarnowiec, Malgorzata. "De zeven zonden van het dienstmeisje: Een moralistische en libertijnse versie beschreven en verbeeld." In *'Tweelinge eener dragt': Woord en beeld in de Nederlanden (1500–1750)*, edited by Karel Bostoen, Elmer Kolfin, and Paul J. Smith, 199–224. Hilversum, 2001.

Schama 1980
    Schama, Simon. "Wives and Wantons: Versions of Womanhood in 17th Century Dutch Art." *Oxford Art Journal* 3, no. 1 (1980): 5–13.

Schama 1987
    Schama, Simon. *The Embarrassment of Riches: An Interpretation of Dutch Culture in the Golden Age*. New York, 1987.

Schölzel 2021–22
    Schölzel, Christoph. "On the Restoration and Painterly Technique of *Girl Reading a Letter at an Open Window* by Johannes Vermeer." In Dresden 2021–22, 195–219.

Seifert 2023
    Seifert, Christian Tico. "Early Ambitions: Vermeer's Journey from Bible to Brothel." In Amsterdam 2023, 126–35.

Smits-Veld 1998
    Smits-Veld, Mieke. "De Muiderkring in beeld: Een vaderlands gezelschap in negentiende-eeuws schilderijen." *Literatuur* 15 (1998): 278–89.

Sneller and Thijs 1993
    Sneller, A. Agnes, and Boukje Thijs. *Jacob Cats Huwelijk*. Amsterdam, 1993.

Suchtelen et al. 2016
    Suchtelen, Ariane van, et al. *Genre Paintings in the Mauritshuis*. The Hague, 2016.

Sutton 1980
    Sutton, Peter C. *Pieter de Hooch: Complete Edition*. London, 1980.

Sutton 2003
    Sutton, Peter C. "Love Letters: Dutch Genre Paintings in the Age of Vermeer." In Dublin and Greenwich 2003–4, 14–49.

Van Boheemen 1989
    Van Boheemen, Petra. "'Hoe men een lief vinden en krygen zal': Ovidius als leermeester." In Apeldoorn 1989, 53–63.

Van Elk 2017
    Van Elk, Martine. *Early Modern Women's Writing: Domesticity, Privacy, and the Public Sphere in England and the Dutch Republic*. New York, 2017.

Van Heemskerck 1626
    Van Heemskerck, Johan. *Minne-kunst, Minne-baet, Minne-dichten, Mengel-dichten*. Amsterdam, 1626.

Van Marion 2005
    Van Marion, Olga. *Heldinnenbrieven: Ovidius' Heroides in Nederland*. Nijmegen, 2005.

Vandivere et al. 2019
    Vandivere, Abbie, et al. "Fading into the Background: The Dark Space Surrounding Vermeer's *Girl with a Pearl Earring*." *Heritage Science* 7, no. 1 (2019): 1–19.

Vergara 1998
    Vergara, Lisa. "'Antiek' and 'Modern' in Vermeer's *Lady Writing a Letter with Her Maid*." In Gaskell and Jonker 1998, 235–55.

Vergara 2003
    Vergara, Lisa. "Women, Letters, Artistic Beauty: Vermeer's Theme and Variations." In Dublin and Greenwich 2003–4, 50–62.

Verdier 1983
    Verdier, Gabrielle. "Gender and Rhetoric in Some Seventeenth-Century Love Letters." *L'Esprit Créateur* 23, no. 2 (1983): 45–57.

Wadum 1998
    Wadum, Jørgen. "Contours of Vermeer." In Gaskell and Jonker 1998, 201–23.

Waiboer 2010–11
    Waiboer, Adriaan E. "'Waarom een Vermer kopen als je ook een Metsu kunt krijgen?': De relatie tussen twee Nederlandse genreschilders." In Dublin, Amsterdam, and Washington 2010–11, 29–51.

Waiboer 2012
    Waiboer, Adriaan E. *Gabriel Metsu, Life and Work: A Catalogue Raisonné*. New Haven and London, 2012.

Waiboer 2023
    Waiboer, Adriaan E. "Elegant Lady Writing at Her Desk." In *The Leiden Collection Catalogue*, edited by Arthur K. Wheelock Jr. et al. 4th ed. New York, 2023–. https://theleidencollection.com/artwork/an-elegant-lady-writing-at-her-desk/.

Washington and Detroit 2004
    Arthur K. Wheelock Jr. et al. *Gerard ter Borch*. Exh. cat. Washington (National Gallery of Art) and Detroit (Detroit Institute of Arts), 2004.

Washington and The Hague 1995–96
    Arthur K. Wheelock Jr. *Johannes Vermeer*. Exh. cat. Washington (National Gallery of Art) and The Hague (Mauritshuis). New Haven and London, 1995–96.

Watteeuw 2015
   Watteeuw, Bert. "Household Names? Domestic Staff in Rubens's Home." In *Rubens in Private: The Master Portrays His Family*, edited by Ben van Beneden, 55–75. Exh. cat. Antwerp (Rubenshuis), 2015.

Weber 1987
   Weber, Gregor. "'t Lof van den Pekelharingh: Von alltäglichen und absonderlichen Heringsstilleben." *Oud Holland* 101 (1987): 126–40.

Weber 1998
   Weber, Gregor. "Vermeer's Use of the Picture-within-a-Picture: A New Approach." In Gaskell and Jonker 1998, 295–307.

Weber 2021–22
   Weber, Gregor J. M. "Cupid in Vermeer's Paintings." In Dresden 2021–22, 125–55.

Weber 2022
   Weber, Gregor J. M. *Johannes Vermeer: Faith, Light and Reflection*. Amsterdam, 2022.

Weber 2023
   Weber, Gregor J. M. "At a Distance." In Amsterdam 2023, 186–91.

Westerbaen 1657
   Westerbaen, Jacob. *Gedichten*. The Hague, 1657.

Westerbaen 1665
   Westerbaen, Jacob. *Den Avond-School voor Vryers en Vrysters om in de Minne-Kunst. . . .* The Hague, 1665.

Wheelock 1995
   Wheelock, Arthur K., Jr. *Vermeer & the Art of Painting*. New Haven, 1995.

Wiedema 2021–22
   Wiedema, Sytske. "Looking at Landscapes: An Interview with Michiel Franken." *RKD Bulletin* 2 (2021–22). https://bulletin.rkd.nl/en/2021-2/looking-landscapes-interview-michiel-franken/.

Wieseman 2017
   Wieseman, Marjorie E. "Inviting Duets." In Paris, Dublin, and Washington 2017, 135–39.

Wieseman 2023
   Wieseman, Marjorie E. "Letters: The World Outside Inside." In Amsterdam 2023, 234–37.

Wolfthal 2013
   Wolfthal, Diane. "Household Help: Early Modern Portraits of Female Servants." *Early Modern Women: An Interdisciplinary Journal* 8 (2013): 5–52.

Wolfthal 2019
   Wolfthal, Diane. "Foregrounding the Background: Images of Dutch and Flemish Household Servants." In *Woman and Gender in the Early Modern Low Countries, 1500–1750*, edited by Sarah Joan Moran and Amanda C. Pipkin, 229–65. Leiden and Boston, 2019.

Zell 2011
   Zell, Michael. "'Liefde baart kunst': Vermeer's Poetics of Painting." *Simiolus* 35, no. 3/4 (2011): 142–64.

INDEX

Page numbers in *italics* refer to illustrations.

Amsterdam, 37, 46–47, 59, 61, 68
Antwerp, 35
Ars Amatoria (*The Art of Love*) (Ovid), 61–64, 72
Astronomer, The (Vermeer), *95*
Avond-School voor Vryers en Vrysters om in de Minne-Kunst, Den (*The Evening School for Single Men and Women in the Art of Love*) (Westerbaen), *62*, 63–64, 72

biblical art. *See* history painting
Bolnes, Catharina, 48–49, 74–75, 78, 91
Bolnes, Willem, 48–49

canal boat service, 14
Caravaggesque works, 82, 84
Cats, Jacob, 58, 64, 74
Christ in the House of Mary and Martha (Vermeer), 35, *36*
citterns, 13, 72, 78, 88, 91
Conste der Minnen, De (Ovid), 61
courts/court culture, 64
courtship: letters of, 50, 58–59, 61–64; manuals for, 61–62; paintings of, 19, 21, 29, 84, 88; and *vrysters* (young single women), 58, 62, 74
Curiosity (ter Borch, Gerard), *70*, 72, 94

de Bray, Salomon and Jan, 64
de Grebber, Maria, 55
de Hooch, Pieter, 25, *27*, 37, *42*, 44, *45*, *69*
de Jongh, Ludolf, 25, *26*
de Knuijt, Maria, 75, 78, 84, 91
de la Serre, Jean Puget, 59
de Lavergne, Gabriel-Joseph, 69
de Scudéry, Madeleine, 59, 68
de Vries, Simon, 45–47
de Wolff, Isabella, 55
Delft, 16, 21, 48–49
Diana and Her Nymphs (Vermeer), 64, *65*
Dircx, Geertje, 35
Dissius, Jacob, 75
Dissius auction catalogue, 37, 75, 78, 84, 91
Dou, Gerrit, 35, *38*, 39
Dutch: emblem books, 21, 88; genre paintings, 14, 32, 35, 44, 64; homes, 32, 72, 82; literacy, 25, 28; marriage practices, 74; mercantile structure, 25; printing/publishing culture, 25; seafaring, 19, 35; society, 25, 37

Elegant Lady Writing at Her Desk (Metsu), 28–29, *31*
Everpoel, Tanneke, 32, 48–49

"Finding of Moses" subject, 94–95
Frick Collection, The, 21, 29, 82, 91

Gerrits, Mary, 49
Girl Interrupted at Her Music (Vermeer), 88, *90*
Girl Reading a Letter at an Open Window (Vermeer), 21, *22*, 23
Girl Receiving a Letter (Metsu), 54, *55*
Girl with a Flute (Vermeer), 82
Girl with a Pearl Earring (Vermeer), 82, *85*
Girl with a Red Hat (Vermeer), 82
Glass of Wine (Vermeer), 88
Griecxser Princerssen, Der (*Greek Princesses, The*) (Ovid), 59
Guitar Player, The (Vermeer), 78, *79*, 91

Hague, The, 14, 62, 64
Hals, Dirck, *16–17*, 19
Heroides (Ovid), 59, *60*, 61, 64, 68
high-life genre painting, 14
history painting, 14, 35, *36*, 64, *65*
Hooft, P. C., 28
Houbraken, Arnold, 28
household servants, 32, 35, 44. *See also* maidservants
Houwelyck (Cats), 58
Huygens, Constantijn, 28, 64

Idle Servant, The (Maes), 37, 40, *41*
inkstands, *19*, 84
Interior with Women by a Linen Cabinet (De Hooch), 37, *42*

Jordaens, Jacob, *34*, 35
Jordis, Henrik, 74
juffrouw (lady), 13, 55, 69, 75, 84, 88, 91, 94

Kenwood, 91

Lady Writing, A (Vermeer), 28–29, *30*, 84

Letter, The (ter Borch, Gerard), *71*, 72

letter-and-maid paintings, 58, 69, 72, 75, 78

letter-and-servant motif, 50, 55

letter-themed paintings: appeal/popularity of, 14, 16, 19, 84; canopied beds in, 72; curtain motif in, 69, 72, 82, 84, 94; focused on listening, 25, *26*; focused on reading, 21, 55, 58, 61; focused on writing, 10, 29, 50, 55, 61, 94; gender and, 75; hallmarks of, 16; *juffrouw* (lady) in, 13; maidservants in, 13, 29, 32, 49, 58; making music and, 29, 88; Ovid's influence on, 64; pairing of ladies and maidservants in, 32, 58; precedents for, 16, 19, 50, 55, 58, 94; as worthy subject matter, 10, 13, 16

Lettres d'une religieuse Portugaise, or *Lettres Portugaises*, 66, *68*, 68–69

literature: amatory, 16, 19; classical, 59–64, 68, 72, 74–75; courtship manuals, 61–62; Dutch emblem books, 21, 88; and emotional expression in Europe, 68; epistolary novel, 69; letter-writing manuals, 58–59, 61–64, 68, 72, 74; love-themed verses, 62–64; on maids, 45–49; moralistic, 58–59; for *vrysters* (young single women), 58, 62, 72, 74; on women in love, 66, 68–69; written by women, 25, 28–29. *See also* songbooks; *specific titles*

Love Letter, The (Vermeer) (cat. 2), *86*, 94; cittern in, 78, 88, 91; composition of, 13, 72; description of, 13, 74, 87–88, 91; details of, *15*; provenance of, 75, 78, 87, 91; seascape in, 19, 88

love/love letters: as central theme, 14; Dutch marriage practices and, 74; female perspective on, 66, 68–69, 74; male perspective on, 66; music and 29; and Ovid's texts, 61, 64; private consumption of 25; role of ladies/servants in, 32, 58; testaments to, 55; Vermeer's focus on 21, 58, 69, 94; and the winds at sea, 16, 19, 58, 88. *See also* literature; women

Maes, Nicolaes, 37, 40, *41*

Maid Asleep, A (Vermeer), 37, *40*

Maidservant at a Window (Dou), 35, *38*, 39

Maidservants: in *Ars Amatoria*, 61; and artists' personal lives, 35; codes of behavior/dress for, 37, 46–47; in Dutch genre paintings, 35; in Dutch homes, 32, 35; and exchange of letters, 13, 63–64, 72, 88; literacy of, 25; literature about, 45–48; market pails (*marketmmers*) and, 46, 50, 58; as models, 49; in prints, *44*; roles of, 32, 35, 44–46, 61, 63–64, 94; social status of, 13, 37, 50; testimony in cases, 48–49; Vermeer's experience with, 32, 48–49; in Vermeer's works, 13, 29, 32, 35, 37, 44–45, 58, 69, 72, 94

Man Reading a Letter to a Woman (De Hooch), 25, *27*

Man Visiting a Woman Washing Her Hands, A (Metsu), 37, 42, *43*

Man Writing a Letter (Metsu), *54*, 55, *56*, 58

maps, 25, 91

maritime travel, 14, 16, 19

Message, The (De Jongh), 25, *26*

Messchert van Vollenhoven family, 91

Metamorphoses (Ovid), 64

Metsu, Gabriel, 28–29, *31*, 37, 42, *43*, *54–57*, 58

Milkmaid, The (Vermeer), 35, 37, *39*, 44–45, 49, 58

Minne-Kunst (*The Art of Love*) (Heemskerk), 62

Mistress and Maid (Vermeer) (cat. 1), *80*, 88, 91, 94; composition of, 13, 29, 69, 72; description of, 13, 74, 81–82, 84; details of, *11*, *33*; infrared image of, 82, *83*; provenance of, 75, 78, 81, 84

mistress-and-maid paintings, 13, 32, 37, 78, 82, 84, 88

Montias, John Michael, 49

Muiderkring (the "Muiden Circle"), 28

music-themed paintings, 13, 21, 29, 72, 78, 88, 91

Netscher, Caspar, 50

Officer and Laughing Girl (Vermeer), 21, *23*

Officer Dictating a Letter, An (ter Borch, Gerard), 72, *73*

Officer Writing a Letter with a Trumpeter (ter Borch, Gerard), 50, *52*, 94

Ovid, 59, *60*, 61–64, 68, 72, 74–75

Painter's Family (Self-Portrait with the Artist's Wife, Catharina van Noort, Daughter Elizabeth, and a Maid), The (Jordaens), *34*, 35

painting-within-a-painting motif, 16, 19, 21, 29, 58, 88, 94–95

Petrarchan love, 72, 74

Portrait of Penelope (Testard), *60*

Princesse Liet-Boec (The Princess Songbook), 59, 61

Rembrandt, 35, 47

Rembrandt Association, 91

Remedia Amoris (*Cures for Love*) (Ovid), 75

Republic of Letters, 28

Rijksmuseum, 19, 74, 91

Roghman, Geertruydt, *44*

Schama, Simon, 44

seascapes, 19, 58, 88

Seated Woman with a Letter (Hals), 16, *17*

Self-Portrait Carving Initials into a Tree (ter Borch, Gesina), *74*, 75

servants. *See* maidservants

Seve Engelen Der Dienst-maagden, De (Seven Angels of Maidservants, The) (Anonymous), *47*, 47–48

Seven Duyvelen Regerende de Hedensdaeghsche Dienst-Maegden (Seven Devils Ruling Present-Day Maidservants) (De Vries), 45, *46*, 47

Soldier Paying a Hostess at an Inn, A (De Hooch), *69*

songbooks, 59, *60*, 61

Stoffels, Hendrickje, 35

Sullerot, Évelyne, 66

Taerling, Hermanus, 49

ter Borch, Gerard, *20*; career of, 64; letter-themed works by, *18*, 19, 50, *52–53*, *70–71*, 72, *73*, *76–77*, 94; models used by, 19, 21, 50, 74–75; portrays Petrarchan love, 72; relationship with Vermeer, 21; staged scenes of, 58, 72, 75, 94

ter Borch, Gesina, 21, *74*, 75

Testard, Robinet, *60*

Thins, Maria, 48–49

van Buyten, Hendrick, 75, 78, 91

van Heemskerk, Johan, 62

van Oosterwijck, Maria, 35

van Ruijven, Pieter, 75, 78, 84, 91

van Schurman, Anna Maria, 28

Vermeer, Johannes: art career of, 14; curtain motif and, 69, 72, 82, 84, 94; death of, 49, 75, 78, 91; Delft home of, 48; description of, 14, 16; fur-trimmed yellow mantle and, 29, 84; experience with his maid, 32, 48–49; family of, 48–49; history paintings by, 35, *36*, 64, *65*; influences on, 35, 44, 64; and *juffrouw*, 13; letter-reader works by, 21, 25; love and courtship themed works of, 21, 29; marriage/wife of, 21, 28–29, 74; models for, 28–29, 32, 37, 49; oeuvre of, 10, 13, 21, 82, 88, 91, 94; optical effects of, 84; Ovid's influence on, 64; patrons of, 75, 78, 84, 91; pearl earrings of, 82, 84; relationship with Ter Borch, 21; tapestry backdrops and, 72, 82; uses dress for status, 37; viewer's position and, 13, 72, 84, 88; wooden coffer prop of, 84

Visscher, Anna Roemers, 28

Visscher, Cornelius, *63*

Visscher, Maria Tesselschade, 28

Westerbaen, Jacob, 62, *63*, 64, 72, 74

Woman Cleaning, A (Roghman), *44*

Woman Drinking Wine and Holding a Letter (ter Borch, Gerard), 75, 77

Woman Holding a Balance (Vermeer), 95

Woman in Blue Reading a Letter (Vermeer), 21, *24*, 25

Woman Reading a Letter (Metsu), 55, *57*, 58

Woman Sealing a Letter with a Maidservant (ter Borch, Gerard), 50, *53*

Woman Tearing up a Letter (Hals), 16, 17, 19

Woman with a Bucket in a Courtyard (De Hooch), 44, *45*

Woman with a Pearl Necklace (Vermeer), 95

Woman with a Wine Glass (ter Borch, Gerard), 75, *76*, 77

Woman Writing a Letter (ter Borch, Gerard), *18*, 19, 21, 94

Woman Writing a Letter with Her Maid (Vermeer) (cat. 3), *92*; composition of, 13, 72; description of, 13, 74, 93–95; details of, *12*, *51*, *67*; provenance of, 78, 91, 93

women: art patrons, 75, 78, 84; artists, 28, 35, 44, 74–75; codes of conduct for, 59; Dutch paintings focus on, 66; education of, 28; of letters, 25, 28–29; moralistic literature for, 58–59; as objects of desire/love, 72; their spaces in homes, 72, 82; Vermeer's focus on, 10, 13, 35, 58. *See also juffrouw* (lady); literature; maidservants

Wyntges, Geertgen, 35

Young Woman at Her Toilet with a Maid, A (ter Borch, Gerard), *20*, 21

Young Woman with a Lute (Vermeer), 88, *89*, 95

IMAGE CREDITS

FIGS. 1 and 9
© GDKE Landesmuseum Mainz
(Ursula Rudischer)

FIG. 6
bpk Bildagentur / Gemäldegalerie Alte Meister /
Staatliche Kunstsammlungen /
Dresden / Wolfgang Kreische /
Art Resource, NY

FIG. 13
© Photographic Archive
Museo Nacional del Prado

FIG. 14
Photo Antonia Reeve

FIG. 15
Photo Studio Tromp

FIGS. 18 and 39
© The National Gallery, London

FIG. 24
Photo Robert Fucci

FIGS. 26 and 36
Courtesy RKD – Netherlands Institute
for Art History, The Hague

FIG. 27
© Musée Fabre de Montpellier
Méditerranée Métropole /
photo Frédéric Jaulmes

FIG. 35
Photo Robert Fucci

FIG. 38
© Royal Collection Enterprises
Limited 2024 |
Royal Collection Trust

FIG. 42
Finnish National Gallery /
Jenni Nurminen

FIG. 43
HIP / Art Resource, NY

FIG. 44
Photo Evan Read

FIG. 48
© RMN-Grand Palais /
Art Resource, NY /
photo Franck Raux

This catalogue is published on the occasion of *Vermeer's Love Letters*,
an exhibition on view at The Frick Collection from June 18 to September 8, 2025.

The exhibition is generously funded by the
Jasmine Charity Trust in memory of Regina Jaglom Wachter.

First published in the United States of America in 2025 by
Rizzoli Electa, a division of
Rizzoli International Publications, Inc.
49 West 27th Street
New York, New York 10001
rizzoliusa.com

Publisher: Charles Miers
Associate Publisher: Margaret Chace
Senior Editor: Philip Reeser
Production Manager: Alyn Evans
Design Coordinator: Tim Biddick
Copy Editor: Christopher Snow Hopkins
Proofreader: Claudia Bauer
Managing Editor: Lynn Scrabis

in association with

The Frick Collection
1 East 70th Street
New York, New York 10021
frick.org

Editor in Chief: Michaelyn Mitchell
Assistant Editor: Gemma McElroy

Designer: Sarah Gifford

Pages 2, 11, and 33: details of *Mistress and Maid* (cat. 1)
Pages 4 and 15: details of *The Love Letter* (cat. 2)
Pages 6–7, 12, 51, and 67: details of *Woman Writing a Letter with Her Maid* (cat. 3)

A CIP catalogue record for this book is available from the Library of Congress.
ISBN: 978-0-8478-4594-1
Library of Congress Control Number: 2024948850

2025 2026 2027 2028 / 10 9 8 7 6 5 4 3 2 1
Printed in China

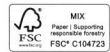